FRIENDS OF GOD

In memory of Pamela Richardson (1936–1992)
a friend of God who first introduced me to
Jesus.

And to 'Pastor' Brian Richardson –
a big smile and a bigger heart.

FRIENDS OF GOD

by

Jeff Lucas

with

Cleland Thom

CROSSWAY BOOKS
NOTTINGHAM

Copyright © 1994 Jeff Lucas
© 1994 Cleland Thom

First edition 1994

All rights reserved.
No part of this publication may be reproduced or transmitted in any form or by any means, electronic, or mechanical, including photocopying, recording, or any information storage and retrieval system, without permission in writing from the publisher.

ISBN 1-85684-058-1

Unless otherwise stated, Scripture quotations in this publication are from the Holy Bible, New International Version. Copyright © 1973, 1978, 1984 International Bible Society. Published in Great Britain by Hodder & Stoughton Ltd.

Typeset by Avocet Typesetters, Bicester, Oxon.

Printed in Great Britain for Crossway Books, Norton Street, Nottingham NG7 3HR, by Cox & Wyman Ltd, Reading, Berkshire.

Contents

Introduction 7

1	Cliff Richard	I'm no hero	9
2	Jim Irwin	The sky's no limit	20
3	Adrian Plass	A smile on the face of God	27
4	R T Kendall	Celebrating discipline	36
5	Nicky Cruz	Once a fighter	44
6	Christine Noble	The discipline of grace	52
7	Clive Calver	A heart for the nation	63
8	Margaret Cundiff	Straight talk, with love	73
9	Gerald Coates	A toast to life	84
10	Sue Rinaldi	Finding God's heartbeat	92
11	Mike and Katey Morris	Two's company	101
12	Fran Beckett	A Father found	110
13	Steve Chalke	Beating the clock	118

A last word 127

Introduction

It was one of those summer Sunday mornings that God created for walks in the parks, picnics and beach parties, but not for church services. Sweltering in the stuffy church building, wrestling with a tie that seemed to be on a mission to strangle me, I tried hard to concentrate on the preacher. Behind him the sun poured down through the coloured windows and dust particles danced furiously in the diffused rays. I wanted to be out in that sun, supernaturally set free from my tie.

I looked at the minister, and immediately felt a warm sense of admiration. What a wonderful man! It was he who had counselled me through my early years as a Christian, unfailingly kind and understanding, oozing wisdom, it seemed, from every pore. He saw things in the Bible that I was totally oblivious to. He always did a good job when he preached, and even though the heat was baking our backs and blurring our minds, he was doing well.

I looked at him again and thought: I'd like to be like him. He appeared to know everything. Quotable prayers dropped from his lips with ease. He and God seemed to be very, very good friends. His wife was wonderful, his children must be perfect. I wanted to be like that. A friend of God, who probably read the Bible through every week and for whom spare time meant prayer time. As the sermon came to an end I considered how good it would be to be like my hero.

Quite a few years later, I find myself frequently standing up doing the preaching these days – and

Friends of God

I've discovered, both from my own experience and from spending time with various Christian leaders from around the world, that walking with God isn't as easy and straightforward as I thought it would be. Twenty years after deciding to make Jesus my best friend, I still fall asleep when I pray and find it difficult to give time to walk with God.

And so I decided to go to a few 'leading' Christians and ask them about their friendship with God. I didn't want to know what they believed about prayer and bible study – I wanted to know what they did in terms of walking with God each day. I knew, for example, that my friend Gerald Coates was against legalistic 'Quiet Times' – the question was, what was he for? What does he actually *do* each day in order to grow closer to the Lord? Are all evangelical leaders getting up at 3 a.m. to pray? Does it get easier?

I asked the questions because I wanted to break the myth that leaders effortlessly walk with God – and I wanted to steal some of their creative ideas! Every one of them was at pains to tell me that 'their way' wasn't at all *the* way. I'm grateful to them all for their time, honesty and helpful suggestions as they have told the truth about what it means to them to be friends of God.

As you read about them, I hope that you will want to go deeper in your own friendship with God as a result.

Jeff Lucas
Chichester 1994

Cliff Richard

I'm no hero

Frequently described as Britain's 'Peter Pan' of rock and roll, Cliff is still at the peak of his popularity after many years in show business. Throughout his career he has remained publicly committed to Jesus Christ.

'**I** think it'd be easier if I ate this with a fork,' exclaimed Cliff Richard, licking his fingers halfway through tucking into a sumptuous cream cake.

Cliff sits in his simple, yet tasteful, Surrey office and speaks to us as though he has known us for five years rather than five minutes. He is warm, open . . . and very secure. And it doesn't take very long to discover that the man who has become the music industry's most evergreen star is equally secure in his relationship with God.

For amid the hype, pretentiousness and greed of that multi-million-pound industry, his simplicity and open-book lifestyle have stood the scrutiny of the public gaze for more than two decades now.

When we met Cliff he was wearing black and white – black trousers and jacket, a black and white James Dean T-shirt and white trainers. And his faith matches his fashion. Black and white. No blurring. And refreshingly simple and uncomplicated.

'Let's put it this way', he says, now finishing off that cream cake with a fork which had been brought in by his secretary. 'I'm fortunate enough to have a wonderful garden at my home in Weybridge. Often when I go outside and wander round I'm immediately aware that I'm actually part of God's creation – and I drift into the "prayer mode". I'm a real romantic!

'That doesn't mean that I fall to my knees on the lawn. But as I walk, I pray and I try to pray precisely and rationally. At other times I'll walk the dogs for an hour and I'll spend the whole time talking to the

Cliff Richard

Lord. But I can't say I've ever really heard his voice in an audible way. Listen, God gave us Jesus, and in doing so he gave us all the physical and tangible evidence we will ever need to prove that he exists. We don't need God to be constantly saying to us, "Turn left at the next set of lights and you'll miss a traffic jam in the high street".

'He gave us Jesus and promised to be our guide. What more do we need? Supposing you are looking for guidance. If you ask God to open a door and it opens – then he's spoken. So go through it! And if it stays shut, then again, he's spoken. So accept that he doesn't want you to go through it. Maybe it's for someone else to go through, or for you to go through later. The trouble is, we all hear what we want to hear. Even when a door's slammed, we still push it'.

As you look round Cliff's office, with rock music playing quietly in the background and the buzz of activity involved in keeping one of the world's greatest pop stars on the road, you are struck by a powerful contrast. On the one hand you see walls decked with gold and platinum discs and other emblems of success. And you get a taste of the fame, adulation and fortune involved in it all. Then you see this man of God with an uncluttered faith and enough humility to thank you for coming along to see him. The two are hard to reconcile. And that's the Cliff charisma: his ability to be one of the world's most respected rock stars – and one of the world's most respected Christians, too. Jesus said it was hard for a rich man to enter the kingdom of heaven. Well, here is one millionaire who has achieved what the camel couldn't do with the eye of a needle.

But it hasn't been easy. Cliff sits casually in his royal blue chair, places his hands upon the oak

Friends of God

conference table and admits: 'The pressure of being in the public eye is enormous. Because of the nature of the press, they would love it if I did something wrong so they could write something horrible about me. They've been trying hard to do that for years. You have every mistake you make paraded before millions, and that's hard. And that kind of publicity doesn't give you much opportunity to respond. It's frightening, sometimes. Surveys show that I'm alongside the Pope, Mother Teresa and Billy Graham as the world's best-known Christian. Imagine the pressure of living with that. It's unbearable at times'.

Cliff's hectic lifestyle, with its endless round of rehearsals, concerts, media events and recording sessions, makes it impossible for him to lead a 'normal' Christian life. There is no Sunday evening service and midweek bible study for him! Going to church can be a nightmare.

'When I go to church I'm clobbered by people I don't want to be clobbered by. The young people are obviously all over me and the older people tend to stand back and give them the chance to meet me – who can blame them? I want to be with people my own age, but I never get to see them'. This 52-year-old is probably too modest to admit that the fact that he looks more like a teenager than someone who is thirteen years away from drawing his pension has something to do with it!

He added: 'I did try wearing disguises once – you know, putting on a hat and things. But I decided that I couldn't get a disguise big enough! I mean, I'd have to get a different nose and everything! Anyway, that's not what church should be about – you shouldn't have to go there anonymously. So I don't often go to church any more. But I do get lots of fellowship. Most of my close friends are

Cliff Richard

Christians, so I get my spiritual input that way. I have people to pray with and advise me – I certainly don't lack fellowship. I probably have more than some churchgoers! It's unorthodox, I know, but God seems to have taken care of me over the years. It's difficult for me to go to church, so church comes to me! After all, church isn't the building you go to, but the people you love and are involved with'.

A story concerning one of Cliff's visits to church gives you an idea of what he is up against. Once he popped into an evening meeting of Pioneer People – formerly Cobham Christian Fellowship – and sat next to a teenager who was a non-Christian visitor. Afterwards, the teenager's friends asked him what he thought of the meeting. 'Rubbish,' said the lad. 'The talk was boring, the music was naff and even worse, I ended up sitting next to this weirdo who was pretending to be Cliff Richard!'

Cliff's unconventional lifestyle has meant that he has had to find some unconventional methods in his devotional life with God. Like many people of his generation, he was brought up on the concept of having a daily quiet time – and like many people, found it difficult to maintain. He chuckled: 'I used to get quite intimidated by stories of these people who got up at 5 a.m. to pray! I mean, I was getting ready to go to bed at 5 a.m., not get up! I eventually realized that it's different for everyone.

'Now I'm not knocking the essence of quiet times if by that you mean that you take time out to spend with God. A quiet time is a good way of describing that. The Bible says we should spend time praying – but it doesn't say when, how long for, or how often. And it can be quite destructive to non-Christians or new Christians if you start making demands on them that they don't feel they can live

Friends of God

up to. I would never want anybody to think that they can't become Christians because they can't make the standard.

'Now if I was a missionary in the Sudanese outback, it'd be different. I'm sure it would be practical to get up early and pray down by the river while it was quiet and cool. But I'm a rock singer, not a missionary, and so I have to adapt my lifestyle accordingly. People are sometimes too quick to pigeon-hole you and expect you to behave like they do. We're all different – different characters, different lifestyles, different ministries. So we can't ever say "This is how to do it." Christianity cannot work like that. Jesus challenged this structured way of thinking all the time'.

So how did Cliff cope in his early Christian life, when he was openly criticized by some sections of the church who thought rock-and-roll was 'of the devil' and who tried to ram the concept of quiet times of the worst sort down his legendary throat?

Again, he laughed. 'For a while, I did what everybody else did – I pretended to have a quiet time. But, like many others, I soon realized that it couldn't be done. Fortunately, being a rock singer gave me an excuse – I was far too busy and had too many schedules to fit it all in. But now I don't have any hang-ups about it. Forcing quiet times upon people is like going back to the Sabbath principle. After all, Sabbath was made for the man, not man for the Sabbath. Quiet times – times with God – are for us. All God wants is for us to give him some time. And anyway, the whole of our lives should be given to him – not just fifteen minutes a day'.

Cliff added: 'If I'm going to stay in this business – and God seems to be using me and telling me that I should stay in it – then I have to face the fact that

Cliff Richard

I can't have a lifestyle like other people. So I have to pray when I can. That might be for a few minutes, or an hour, or not at all. I have tried using lists of people to pray for at times – people like my family, friends and non-Christians who work for me: only three out of my fourteen staff are Christians. Their salvation is important to me. But I'm not using lists at the moment. I have to be flexible. What works one week when I'm recording an album in Britain won't work the next week when I'm touring abroad'.

Although Cliff is flexible in his prayer life, he is, however, far more disciplined in his reading of scripture. He decided many years ago that he needed a regular intake of the Bible and has always done his best to achieve this goal. He tends to read at night – and prays before he starts that he'll stay awake and actually absorb what he's reading! After a busy day in the studios or on tour, he finds it easy, like the rest of us, to let the word of God wash straight over him.

Perhaps surprisingly, for someone who is quite modern in his approach to the Christian life, Cliff prefers to use the Revised Standard Version of the Bible. He loves the poetic nature of the translation and he reckons that, 'Even Solomon in all his glory was not arrayed like one of these' sounds far richer than the Good News Bible's 'Even Solomon with all his wealth did not have clothes as beautiful as some of these flowers' (Mt. 6:28).

But within a framework of disciplined bible reading, Cliff's selection of which passages to read tends to reflect his spontaneous, artistic temperament. He often opens the Bible at random and reads the first book he sees. When we interviewed him he was studying the New

Friends of God

Testament again (Philippians) and was vibrantly excited about discovering new truths from passages he knew really well.

He said: 'Whether you know a passage well or not, it's inevitable that you will pick up something new from it. God knows we don't know it all. If we are prepared to accept that there's always something new to learn, then God will also be there to show us and give us fresh revelation'.

Cliff admits to a common problem – remembering bible verses off by heart. The man who can recall a thousand songs and who has learnt the scripts of musicals really struggles to memorize scriptures. 'My mind focuses on the present,' he says. 'I can learn something off by heart quite quickly and retain it for a while. But then my mind will go off onto the next thing and I'll forget it'.

Cliff does find, though, that the Holy Spirit helps him to remember whole chunks of scripture when he needs to. He and his friend Bill Latham do question-and-answer presentations around the country and during them Cliff will often find himself reciting a relevant passage almost word for word. He couldn't tell you where to find it, but invariably, when he checks back with the original text, he finds he remembered it correctly – much to his relief!

The Bible tends to be Cliff's favourite book; he's not an avid reader, and finds that the message of most Christian books is the same, with just the approach being different. Tapes feature more prominently in Cliff's life – he enjoys listening to David Pawson's teaching tapes at home and in his car after becoming a fan of David's while attending Millmead Baptist Church in Guildford.

Cliff's straightforward approach to Christianity doesn't leave too much room for doubt – which

Cliff Richard

is why his public communication of the gospel has resulted in thousands of people becoming Christians over the years.

He says: 'No, I don't doubt God very often – if ever. How could I? Early in my Christian life I used to become frustrated worshipping somebody I couldn't see, and I used to wish like mad there was something physical to get hold of. But we need to go back to the fact that the most tangible thing has already happened – Jesus came and lived on the earth. We don't need anything else! We must be at peace about it all and realize we aren't going to see him this side of the Second Coming. If we ever doubt God's existence, we must remember that we've got history and archaeology on our side – they all prove Jesus' existence'.

Surprisingly, despite Cliff's unashamedly strong faith and enormous profile as a Christian, he's never led anybody to Christ on a one-to-one basis. But, as ever, he is quite secure about his gifting and how it must operate.

'I don't think I'll ever lead anyone, individually, to the Lord – it just wouldn't be possible. Obviously, with my lifestyle, it's not easy to have a day-to-day relationship with my fans and the general public, and there's the danger of them following Jesus because I do, rather than because they have met him for themselves. But on the other hand, many people have become Christians in my gospel concerts, which is brilliant. Even then, I have to be careful that they're making a genuine decision. When you're very well known and have a large following, especially among young people, fans tend to copy what you do. So I leave it to local churches to follow people up if they've made a response in a meeting. It's far healthier that way'.

Friends of God

Cliff is someone who continues to confound his critics. He is still getting chart hits years after his contemporaries have retired. He continues to look young when many men of his age are bald and have pot-bellies. And he's still living clean in an industry not exactly known for its morality. People who wait for him to age, fade or fall wait on. But he doesn't find any of it easy. He needs people – people like you and me – to pray for him.

He says: 'In some ways, the pressure is not as strong as it used to be. In the early days many sections of the church were hostile towards me, whereas that doesn't often happen now. And I'm sure that one of the reasons the pressure is not so acute is because more and more people are praying for me. It does make a difference. And I desperately need that prayer cover to continue and increase.

'It used to annoy me when people said they were praying for me. I used to think "Huh, I don't need your prayers!" That was because I reckoned they thought there must be something wrong with me! I used to think you only prayed for people because they were horrible!

'But I think I've learned a few lessons since then. I do need people's prayers. They need to pray for me that I have the physical strength to keep up the pace. I'm doing more now than I was when I was eighteen, and that can be tough at times. And they need to ask God to protect me from the things the devil throws at me. He'd love to bring me down if he could. Yes, do please ask people who read *Friends of God* to pray for me. That's important'.

Get the message? Despite what the papers say, this super-star who is seemingly immune to old age, to pride and to the moral corruption that has destroyed many Christians in the public eye is humble enough

Cliff Richard

and honest enough to know his limitations. He knows he needs your prayers. He's in it – with you.

With them, he can carry on, not just delighting grannies and teenagers alike with his music, but being God's man in the music industry. And influencing the lives of millions with that simplicity, that warmth and that openness.

Jim Irwin

The sky's the limit

Colonel James Irwin became a space hero when he took part in the first Apollo voyage to land on the moon. He returned more determined to serve the Lord, and with his wife Mary founded the High Flight Foundation in Colorado Springs. Jim Irwin died in 1991 while out jogging near his home. Mary continues the work and mission of High Flight.

Jim Irwin

Late at night, a long way from home, you are driving down a dark, lonely country lane, and the unthinkable happens – your car splutters, coughs – and dies. A sickly feeling in your stomach and the night seems very black as you ponder the fact that you are 'miles from anywhere'.

Apollo astronaut Jim Irwin suffered a vehicle malfunction once – and he was a very long way from home at the time! Neither the RAC nor the AA answer requests for help from the moon! Home was so distant that Jim recalls being able to block out planet Earth from view by merely holding up his thumb, as he stood on the farthest frontier ever travelled by man.

One of only a handful of human beings ever to stand on the lunar surface, he became aware that there was a mechanical problem with the steering of his lunar 'rover', the vehicle that enabled Irwin to take a six mile, four hour drive on the moon. Irwin decided to pray. Hadn't Jesus declared, 'I am with you always' – presumably that included the moon? The next morning, it was steering perfectly – and as his wife Mary says, 'Only God knows why it worked the next morning when neither Jim or his fellow astronauts had worked on it . . .'

Another mechanical problem hit when Jim tried to erect the 'ALSEP' – the Apollo Lunar Surface Experiments Package. ALSEP was a sophisticated miniature space station full of scientific instruments; it was designed to be left on the moon to measure solar wind and other data, and then relay the data

Friends of God

back to earth. Jim couldn't get the station erected – a problem had developed with some small pins which required some fine adjustment – difficult with huge space gloves on! In addition to this, the astronauts work plan on the lunar surface was timed carefully to the minute, and they were already behind schedule. Irwin said, 'I prayed to God to show me the right way. The answer was to get down on one knee, supporting myself with one hand while I took the pins out with the other hand . . . when I released them all, the central station erected itself – it all popped up, three feet high'. I imagine that the sense of relief was considerable!

But, then, high drama on the lunar surface was but one of many tense, death-defying moments for Jim Irwin. For years he risked life and limb as a test pilot, while a colonel in the airforce. His adventurous, enquiring spirit led him on unusual expeditions, including numerous trips to Mount Ararat to try to find Noah's Ark.

But adventure was not Irwin's god. Lunar travel was not the climax of his life. Jim had a favourite saying, which summed up the real heartbeat of his life: 'Jesus Christ walking on earth is more important than man walking on the moon'.

With this in mind, I expected to discover a loud, extrovert evangelistic character when I met Jim Irwin briefly a couple of years ago: a Christianized 'Indiana Jones', but I was in for a shock. A slight man, with a quiet, unassuming manner but a broad, winning smile, he did not fit the caricature of a modern-day swashbuckling explorer. He was a man of depth rather than volume, who rarely articulated his thoughts even to those nearest and dearest to him. His beautiful wife Mary (she was a professional model – and it shows!) told me that she felt that

Jim Irwin

she only ever really knew what was in Jim's heart either when they prayed together, or when he wrote to her. He preferred reading to talking: someone had told him, 'In five years from now you'll be the same person as you are now – apart from the influence of the books that you read, and the people that you meet'. Irwin took the advice to heart and as Mary puts it, 'He read voraciously; wherever he was, there was a book'. And his favourite work was *the* Book. He had a reading rack attached to his exercise bicycle so that during his morning physical workout he could feed his heart and mind with the pure truth of Scripture. On average, he would read through the Bible once every year – originally he used the King James Version, but later switched to the New International. 'Bible reading notes' played no part in his disciplines – he would just pick a book and read through it. Not that his love for the Scriptures was always a blessing to his family: Mary describes the times when 'Jim would insist on reading the Bible to the family. The only trouble was that he sometimes made it about as exciting as reading a dictionary'. Nevertheless, she still looks back on those family times, and particularly the times when she and Jim would kneel at the bedside with hands joined together in prayer, with almost reverent affection. 'Those times of prayer were such precious times – to be honest, they were so few because of the hectic travelling schedule that was Jim's life – they were never enough'.

Surprisingly, perhaps, for such a thoughtful man, Jim kept no spiritual journals and he was not a person who fasted frequently either. Though Mary recalls one time when their eldest daughter was experiencing some personal difficulties, and that drove Jim to prayer with fasting. But his walk with

Friends of God

God meant that he lived in a state of preparedness: 'Before he preached he would have no concentrated times of prayer, simply because he seemed to always be in an attitude of prayer'.

But what of action in terms of ministry and Christian service? I was keen to know about the days *after* Apollo – was life an anticlimax after that epic adventure? Mary enthused: 'Not at all. Jim began a ministry which we are still continuing today. When he went to the moon he took with him a silk flag from every nation of the world, and then brought them back, and committed himself to go to the head of state of every nation as a goodwill ambassador – but also to share the gospel of Christ with them too'. This passion for the nations was worked out in his prayer life too. When the Berlin Wall fell and when other historic events developed, he would often speak of the happening as 'an answer to prayer'. There was vision closer to home as well. Jim had a great burden for families splintered by marital breakdown, so he and Mary initially organized and paid for a number of military families to attend a conference designed especially to help. 'Miracles were done that week – God literally put families back together. It was the beginning of a vision that still lives with us. Jim wanted to build a huge centre especially to allow couples to come for help, counsel, and prayer'.

So was there a chink in the warrior's armour? Did he ever doubt his faith? Mary smiled. 'I don't think that Jim ever really seriously doubted that God was there – he had a real trust in a Heavenly Father. If he doubted anything, it was himself. Sometimes Jim would experience fears and feelings that he was unworthy, that he hadn't done quite enough to serve God, that his best was not good enough. I feel that

Jim Irwin

there were times when he was driven, spurred on by guilt, regretful over the earlier years of his life when, despite the strong influence of his godly mother, he didn't live for the Lord'.

Jim Irwin took his last high flight on 8th August, 1991. Just as he prepared himself in quarantine at Cape Canaveral for the moon flight in 1968, so he methodically seemed to prepare himself to cross the final frontier – even though his death came as an apparent surprise. He confided in his good friend, Nicky Cruz, with whom he had shared many prayers, 'I have only got two or three years left.' And then, just before his death, which came quickly during a cycling trip in the Colorado Montains, he began to approach others, telling one friend 'I need to tell you goodbye – I won't be seeing you again'. In those days before the journey, Jim called everybody who had been close to him, even left messages on their telephone answering machines, expressing just how important and special they had been to him. Could it be that the quiet, even 'frustrating' introvert overcame something of a barrier within himself at the very end of his life – an adventurer to the last?

Almost uncannily, Mary felt that God was preparing her too for Jim's departure. She found herself reading a book by Catherine Marshall, herself a widow, entitled *To Live Again*, and felt that the Lord was speaking to her, making her ready.

Fittingly, Jim's funeral was a resounding testimony to the grace of God. Mary's eyes glowed as she described the day. 'There was such a sense of God's peace, God's concern expressed for us all. And more than a dozen people made decisions to follow Christ at the service'.

I ended my interview with Mary Irwin, and left

Friends of God

her sitting in the busy offices of 'High Flight', the walls hung with pictures of the lunar surface, colour portraits of her and Jim dining with Presidents, a ministry that continues. She had told me how she felt that day when she looked up at the moon with the knowledge that her husband was up there, standing on that distant globe in the night. 'I had such a sense of deep peace that I had to kneel down before God, and praise Him for the fact that Jim was going to come back to me safely – it was such a peace that I couldn't begin to comprehend it'.

As I hugged Mary goodbye, I had a sense that she knew that Jim was 'out there with God', having conquered the last enemy of us all by standing in the shadow of the pioneer of our faith, Jesus.

And that the peace of God was still with her.

Adrian Plass

A smile on the face of God

The best-selling Sacred Diary was first published in 1986. Now Adrian is the author of eleven books and travels and speaks widely.

A pile of sealed brown envelopes sits squarely on the desk, each one with a name on the front, like an ominous stack of unpaid bills. There are no stamps; none are necessary, for this is mail in God's in-tray. Adrian reaches out and lifts one of them up, as if offering it up to the ceiling, and begins to pray.

Each envelope contains a letter written to God about a situation or a person and each time Adrian waves it in the general direction of heaven, he's saying, 'Here you are Lord – we've talked about this one before. Action please!' One envelope is reserved for those people whom Adrian considers his enemies. 'Course, I don't really want to pray for them at all, or I want to pray, "Lord, let 'em die and let me be there to see it!" But as I lift up my enemy envelope and do my best to ask God to drop some blessing on those that I'd naturally like to drop something else on, I feel my own attitude softening. My children would love to look inside and see whose names are in that one!'

Adrian Plass writes what many of us are thinking, but are too scared to actually say. Perhaps we've sat in silent agony through church services that featured ridiculous prophecies, archaic religious language, and over-zealous and unreal super-spirituality. We've wanted to protest, but fear and peer pressure silenced us. Adrian broke that silence, initially with his *Sacred Diary of Adrian Plass*. It was as if a collective sigh of relief (and a deafening roar of laughter) was heard throughout the wooden panelled corridors of evangelicalism: nearly 250,000 copies were sold. The book was hilarious, but perhaps its appeal was due to something far deeper: Adrian managed to poke fun without wounding; ask questions without descending into destructive cynicism, mainly because he made himself vulnerable in the process. His own character in the book is a lovable, clumsy man who tends to get a little proud when asked to 'do things in the church', and who has an eye for pretty girls. And the bestselling trend has continued – he is currently writing his eleventh book.

So where does the ability to communicate the goodness of God come from? Has Plass climbed up to a pinnacle of spirituality, and from that vantage point is now able to help us lesser mortals to know God better? In some ways, the opposite is true. A nervous breakdown eight years ago, when everything in his life seemed to crumble apart, was the beginning of a whole new friendship with God. 'My breakdown brought me to a point where I had to stop my posturing and posing as a Christian. Prior to that praying had been a prison of performance for me; I was brought up with the idea that there are four types of person who are surely bound for hell: those who violate copyright laws (particularly with reference to overhead transparencies), those who refuse to read *Buzz* magazine (forerunner of *Alpha*), those who have a problem with masturbation – and those who don't have quiet times . . .

'When everything in me collapsed, I began to learn that prayer is actually friendship – it is being with someone rather than just doing something. Now I talk to God all the time: moaning about things, shouting, chatting to him softly and warmly, unloading my anxieties . . .

Friends of God

'Most days I begin by sitting at my typewriter, perhaps with some music playing in the background and reading something from the Bible, often a Psalm. I like to use the Jerusalem Bible, it's beautifully written, so clear, but so elegant. Loads of people have told me that I really should use the New International Version – so much so that I almost feel like holding up a clove of garlic to it!

'The best part of that morning time is when I just say nothing, and allow God's presence to seep through me. I find that to be a time when I am warmed, emotionally and mentally. To fully describe it is impossible, it's difficult to wrap it all up in words. All I know is that there is a great sense that this person who I call God cares for me so totally, and I occasionally find myself literally pushed down onto my knees by the weight of that love; it's a good weight. I look forward to those times . . . they're almost . . . edible.

'Of course, there are other times when I'm too busy with "important" things, or feeling disillusioned. Prayer is a bit like dieting. I know it's good for me, and I feel good when I do it, but sometimes other distractions come'. He has learned to be honest with God during the tough times, expressing just exactly how he feels. If anything, one of his greater challenges is being honest about his feelings with other Christians: 'I don't want to be an edited version of myself, I want to be me, but I don't want to hurt anybody in saying what I feel. Sometimes I feel locked in, unable to communicate on certain issues. I write poems that could never be published because they could offend, but I honestly believe that the rawness of them could help hurting people'.

The breakdown also taught Adrian to be a little

easier on himself, and to realize that the ebb and flow of his emotions are not all a barometer reading on his relationship with God. 'I used to believe that everything that I felt had a spiritual root – and I would drive myself mad trying to find it, wondering if God was saying something, or telling me that I was doing something wrong. Now I know that I'm a person distinct, in that sense, from God. I get tired. Things get boring. Life doesn't always go my way, I get fearful or insecure. But I don't have to go on a hunt for a cause for every effect in my life. Some days will be bad. But as my friend, Stuart Henderson says, "All gigs pass!" '

The pain of the past means that Adrian is delighted by others who major on the victorious side of the Christian life, but he feels a calling to try to bring some sense and comfort to those who are feeling lost in the shadows. 'In Christ, God has come down as low as he can get, to where we are, not joining in with our sin, but getting down alongside us in the mud and the mire and showing a way out. I want my writing to get to where people are – to get alongside them, not shout down a well at them'.

The Sacred Diary was originally written as therapy for Adrian as he recovered from his collapse. In it he hilariously wrote about bizarre revelations and visions that Christians claim to have received from God. So does *he* hear from the Almighty?

'I think that we create problems for people when we declare so quickly that it's definitely God speaking to us. I certainly feel that God teaches me things in a number of different ways. Sometimes it's a kind of imaginary conversation that goes on inside my head. Like when I went to South Africa recently. I was feeling a bit depressed about going, and as I

Friends of God

sat in our kitchen having a good old moan to God about it, a conversation began inside my head . . .

'I said, "God, I don't want to go to South Africa. Being necklaced and killed isn't in my medium- or even long-term planning". A question surfaced in my thoughts.

"Why have they asked you to go?"

"Well, to cheer them up".

"What's wrong with that then?"

"Nothing, I suppose".

"Go, but don't tell them off. Tell them what you know about me".

"All right then".

'Now I can't categorically say that God said those things to me, but I will go so far as to say that I learned through that mental conversation, and I certainly felt a whole lot better about going after that little internal chit-chat'.

Adrian also believes that God has a lot to say to us through creation – and through the daily unfolding of life's circumstances. 'There are parables in the bones of the world – I'm always learning lessons from ordinary things'.

Not that he is suggesting that the voice of God is only to be heard in the colours of the rainbow/splash of the sunset/crashing of the waves upon the beach. God seems to talk to him through very ordinary events – such as rides in tube trains.

'I was on my way to speak at yet another meeting, thinking, "What on earth am I doing, messing around with my little carrier bag full of books . . . ?"

'I felt very insignificant, the need to *be* somebody was strong. A couple of rather plummy-voiced city gents got on the train, real high-fliers, and that only served to make me feel more valueless and inferior. There they were, chatting about their stocks and gilts and market reports and there I sat clutching my plastic bag thinking, "I want to be like them".

'Suddenly the train arrived at Baker Street station, and one of them jumped up and announced "Oh no! – We've been going the wrong way!"

'I was very, very pleased about this – and then as they hopped off, all city sophistication gone, I realized – yes, with their value system the way it is, they *are* going the wrong way. Again, no booming voices, but God taught me something through that incident'.

I wanted to press the point further – had there never been a voice from the sky?

'Not an audible voice, but there have been times when a voice inside my mind spoke out so strongly that it stopped me dead in my tracks'.

One time he was praying for a young man who was about to go to college to train for the Anglican ministry. 'Suddenly something in my head said "He's got a building society account". I thought, "This is madness, but I'd better say something before I bottle out". So I said to the young man, "You've got a building society account, haven't you?" He flushed immediately. In filling out his grant application forms, he hadn't declared the money that he had saved – and put in the building society . . . it was a potential cover-up job . . .

Talking of covering up – does he ever try it? 'Well, one of my latest temptations is my ability to appear humble in public when people say nice things about me. I've mastered the technique pretty well now. I can look amazingly lowly even though inside I'm sporting this massive great big head about myself!'

As he was being so honest, I thought I'd ask him about any challenges that he has with prayer.

Friends of God

'I'd like to pray *more* with Brigit and my children – and *less* in those prayer meetings before church services, which I am seriously allergic to'.

He went on to explain that he struggles with the mandatory 'times of prayer' (we Christians seem to have 'times' of everything) where everyone gathers round to pray for the speaker prior to a service. 'I'd far rather stand at the back of a meeting and just observe, get the feel of things. I'm never quite sure what to do during those prayer times. Everyone seems to be springing up and down on their heels and murmuring things. A few months ago in Australia I had an awful experience. There was a bloke praying very loudly right next to me and he kept yelling "Jeee-eeesus!!" and I got an earful of spit. I tried my best to make agreeable mooing noises ("Mmmmmmm Lord") but in the end could stand no more so I beat a hasty retreat and dashed to the loo. Once inside, I felt safe, and said to God, "Stay close, here we go again . . ." '

But like most busy Christians, he could do with more family prayer. 'I don't know why it is that most Christian couples seem to feel a measure of insecurity about being spiritually naked in front of one another, when we feel quite happy about being stark naked physically!' He declares an 'enormous respect' for Brigit, because 'most of the time, she is right in what she says – regretfully . . .'

And what of guidance – and the future?

Adrian has developed a simple approach to guidance and the will of God – again, for the sake of personal survival. 'I used to believe that I would be ill-advised to cross a road if I had not had a prayer meeting beforehand – and I was emotionally paralysed as a result. Some people are into power healing – I was into power steering! But when I look at people like Paul the apostle, I don't see this nail-biting complexity. He was in an attitude of prayer constantly, took common-sense decisions, and occasionally got stopped in his tracks by the odd dream or vision that clarified the direction that God wanted him to go.

'As for my own future, I suppose my major fear would be that I might start churning out stuff that's no longer significant – but I do feel fairly safe about what's ahead. Brigit says that I'm ludicrously spoilt by God, and new things are opening up all the time. Whatever's up ahead, I do know that I will probably always walk with something of an emotional limp . . .'

Perhaps he will. But his pen has made us laugh, cry and think. God has used Adrian Plass to speak to the rest of us who also struggle and hobble along – to let us know that as we keep going forward, we do so in the Father's love.

R. T. Kendall

Celebrating discipline

An American living in London, R. T. Kendall is a prolific author and popular bible teacher. He is also the Senior Pastor of Westminster Chapel.

Westminster, London. Home to the Houses of Commons and Lords, centres of national power, Big Ben, captured on a million postcards, a symbol of London recognized worldwide. Westminster Abbey, the final resting place of Kings and Queens. In the tree-lined square, one of Britain's more recent famous sons, Sir Winston Churchill, captured and still now as a bronze statue looking ever resolute. And in the middle of all this is Westminster Chapel, the church originally made famous by the expository genius of Dr. Martyn Lloyd-Jones, the man who spent a decade or two preaching his way through just one book of the Bible.

The present minister of the Chapel is Dr. R. T. Kendall (I have no idea what the initials stand for – everybody seems to know him simply as 'R.T.!'). An American by birth, he is one of Britain's most renowned bible teachers, often thrilling thousands at events like Spring Harvest with his punchy and challenging bible studies. He is internationally respected, the author of fourteen books – and, as we meet to talk about his relationship with God, he is somewhat nervous.

His anxiety surfaces because, as we settle down to talk about his obvious disciplines, he is concerned that he might give an impression of 'super-spirituality'. He is worried that the details of his prayer life might discourage others because they don't have the same daily pattern. Or perhaps they might be tempted to lift up R.T. as someone special.

Friends of God

Like most friends of God, he is wary to boast about anything or anybody except Jesus.

When I listen to his daily routine, I begin to understand his concern, because of all the people whom I interviewed, he had the most rigid disciplines, rising early and spending a full two hours every day, between 7 a.m. and 9 a.m., praying and reading scripture. He is quick to point out that this is a time for him personally – he refuses to do any sermon preparation during this early session. 'Other people have to go to work at 9 a.m., and so do I, so I don't think that it's appropriate for me to use that time to work'.

Already I feel myself shrinking with intimidation, and, to be honest, feeling unsure about this prayer/work approach to life. But I shelve my own reactions – what does R.T. do with that two-hour time?

'I go into the living room of our home, and begin by saying the Lord's prayer. Then I pray for the blood of Christ to cleanse my mind, my spirit and my body, welcoming the Holy Spirit into my life for that day. Two specific scriptures have become very important to me as I begin my prayer time: one is Hebrews 4:16, because it calls me to draw close to my heavenly Father with a strong sense of confidence, "Let us then approach the throne of grace with confidence, so that we may receive mercy and find grace to help us in our time of need"; and the other is 1 John 4:16, which speaks so powerfully of the reality that I can dwell in the love of God. "And so we know and rely on the love God has for us. God is love. Whoever lives in love lives in God, and God in him."

'And then I spend a lot of time thanking God for everything that I can think of. I try to recount all the events that I experienced the previous day, listing them methodically, and then I give thanks to the Lord. I believe that God wants us to learn to be thankful for even the tiniest things . . .'

And then R.T. quotes another scripture, this time Philippians 4:6, 'Do not be anxious about anything, but in everything, by prayer and petition, with thanksgiving, present your requests to God'. This man of the book seems to have a scripture for everything, even when I ask him if his mind tends to wander when he's praying.

'Oh yes, that happens a lot, sometimes because I'm tired, sometimes because I feel a sense of warfare and oppression from the enemy. It's so easy for the mind to drift, particularly as I rarely pray out loud. I take comfort from Psalm 16:8. (I nod knowingly at this point, feeling the need to give the impression that I know every verse of all 150 Psalms off by heart. Probably he isn't convinced by my little performance, because he quotes it anyway!)

'I have set the LORD always before me. Because he is at my right hand, I shall not be shaken.' He goes on to explain: 'The Psalmist had to *set* God before him, fix his heart and mind upon the Lord. I have to do that too, and I think about the fact that Jesus is sitting there with me as I pray. After all, by his Spirit, he is there!'

This disciplined approach to life is something that R.T. learned from his father, who made an indelible impression upon him. 'My dad had a very strong prayer life. Before he retired he would spend thirty minutes each day – but in later years and with more time, he would spend between one and two hours on his knees. I have always been impressed by people, preachers particularly, who know how to pray. Writers like Brother Lawrence, *Practising the presence of God*, and E. M. Bounds, who wrote a series of books on prayer which are now classics, have stirred and inspired me'.

'Methodical' seems to be the byword for the doctor in just about everything that he does. He writes a personal spiritual journal every day. He reads through the Bible (New International Version) once each year, using the 'McCheyne' reading plan, which takes you through the Old Testament once each year, and the Psalms and the New Testament twice annually. And he has a prayer list of over 200 items (yes, 200!) which he works through every day – even when at Spring Harvest! I was gasping by this point – and so he made me feel a little better (though only slightly) by telling me that he cuts the list down to an abridged version when he is on holiday! 'I have the list, but I don't treat it as a list. I try to go through and pray for the people and issues each day as if I had never ever prayed for them before'.

If it all sounds a little tiresome, R.T. is quick to dispel the idea that he is ensnared by his routine: 'Of course, I do get tired sometimes, and tiredness creates a feeling of boredom. But I want to live my life out of discipline, not just for what is fun, or for what I feel like doing'. The morning is definitely his preferred time for this meeting with God: 'It works for me, but if you're not a morning person, then pick a better time that suits you. I'm also one who is early to bed – usually by 9.45 p.m.'.

And he is anxious to rule out the notion that prayer is something reserved for a special time during the day. 'God hears us whenever and wherever we pray, and sometimes comes up with swift and unusual answers. Last year, my wife, Louise, and I arranged to meet my 84-year-old father in Orlando, Florida, at a particular hotel. Only when we arrived there and were driving down the freeway did we realize that there were four hotels all with the same name in that large city which literally teems with tens of thousands of people. We were very nervous that my father could end up in difficulty if he was unable to find us – the sun was burning hot that day.

'We found ourselves driving down the main street, stuck in a traffic jam, bumper to bumper. I turned to Louise and said, "Let's ask God to help us to see where dad is right now", so we quickly prayed together in the car. Suddenly, as we drove by a car park, Louise cried out, "There he is!" I seriously believe that the odds against that happening were millions to one: thank God for his interest in the details'.

And not only does he believe in being specific in prayer, but in being honest as well. 'I feel that we should be totally real about what we are feeling when we talk to God. After all, he knows anyway; Psalm 51:6 declares that the Lord wants reality: "Surely (God) desires truth in the inner parts".'

And so I nudged towards the question that I was just dying to ask: what about the supernatural? Is there room in the methodical doctor's orderly private world for the spontaneous, for revelation, for the surprising God?

'Most of the time God speaks to me through scripture, but yes, there have been a number of times when I have heard the voice of God. I cannot say that it was audible, but it was every bit as clear as an audible voice. I must say, though, that I could probably count those times on both hands down through the years. The most dramatic encounter with God for me happened back in 1955, on

Friends of God

October 31st to be precise. It was like a Damascus Road experience. I could hear a conversation going on between Jesus and the Father – one said, "He wants it" – and the other replied "He can have it!". Suddenly, I felt as if a flame of peace filled my being, and for about a minute I saw the face of Jesus – it was so vivid that I can still remember that face today, thirty-eight years later'.

R.T. is excited as he recounts the story – and then starts to worry again: 'Perhaps I shouldn't have told you about that, it could give the wrong impression to people and they could feel let down if they haven't had similar encounters'. The man really has a deep concern about the effect of his words on people – a good quality for a preacher.

As if eager to convince me of his own frailty, he tells me that there are times when he battles with doubts. 'God's word to us is a promise, but that means that there will be times when we doubt the promise. During those times I endeavour to just stand my ground, to stand firm on the evil day, as Paul encourages the Ephesians to do.

'I struggle with personal insecurity, particularly after I have preached. I want to do well, to do my best, and I need affirmation and encouragement. If all has gone well in preaching, then I feel exhausted, but it's a pleasant exhaustion. If I have done badly, then it's painful! But I tend to just give it to God, call it a bad day, and move on . . .'

When it comes to preaching, R.T. doesn't like arriving early to meetings. 'If I'm speaking at 7.30 p.m., the ideal time to arrive as far as I'm concerned is 7.29 p.m.! I don't like to be distracted, and find settling into meetings quite exhausting.

'When I first got started, I used to accept every invitation that came my way. Now, I pray about each invitation, and if I don't feel positive and right about it, I won't go'.

Our time together was over – R.T. had a busy schedule, and also was eager to get back to his room for another time with God, and another look through the inevitable list. Although I'm not convinced that I could follow R.T.'s pattern, I know that he finds God in it, and that he genuinely finds his disciplines liberating. One phrase from R.T. lingered in my mind after we parted. 'I'd rather pray than do anything'. May God give all of us a heart like that.

Nicky Cruz

Once a fighter

Nicky Cruz used to be a vicious gang leader and street fighter. His story is told by David Wilkerson in The Cross and the Switchblade *and also in his own book* Run Baby Run. *Nicky continues an international evangelistic ministry based in Colorado Springs.*

The smash-hit movie *The Cross and the Switchblade* depicted him as a wild, angry street fighter. He was the son of a Puerto Rican voodoo priestess who told her child that she hated him when he was just eight years old.

He was the thug who waved a dagger and spat obscenities in David Wilkerson's face, but whose rage was later melted by the love of Jesus.

Meeting Nicky Cruz in his comfortable offices in snowbound Colorado Springs was a surprise. I was one of millions who were thrilled by his first book, *Run Baby Run*, which was standard reading for all Christians in the Seventies – and is still a prescribed school text-book in a number of Latin American countries.

Perhaps I expected to still find a muscular teenager with a gang jacket and a red scarf tied round his forehead, as portrayed in that film, as if time stands still for heroes! Instead I was greeted by an agile 52-year-old – he runs five miles every day, and, from the looks of him, could still take care of himself on the streets!

Nicky remains a fighter. He is still a joyful, angry, unpredictable and passionate man, tender when he talks about God, scathingly furious when he talks about the hypocrisy of some of the media mega-ministries, refreshingly honest when he talks about himself. He was exhausted when we met, having just flown back from a heavy crusade schedule in Finland; I sneaked a look at the year planner on his

Friends of God

office wall, which depicted a crammed packed schedule of globetrotting.

With such a demanding schedule, Nicky has to know about the power of prayer – even the SOS type. For example, when he flew into Angola and his airplane was riddled by seventeen bullets and started to go down, Nicky's prayer at the time shows the solid-rock peace he has with God: 'Well, Lord, this is it'. Another 'quickie' was prayed the first time he spoke to a packed crowd in London's Royal Albert Hall. His interpreter got sick (back then Nicky spoke very little English – his accent is still very strong), and so as he walked to the platform he muttered, 'Well, Jesus, here I go, please help me . . .' So convinced is he in the power of prayer that he has occasionally travelled with seventy intercessors – and needed every one of them! During one Latin Crusade, he was preaching on 'Satan on the loose' in a football stadium packed with 45,000 people. Two thousand witches attended the meeting, cursing Nicky and daubing blood all over the arena where the crowds were gathered. A large black cloud gathered over the stadium in an otherwise blue, clear sky. Nicky felt depressed and troubled as darkness filled the entire arena for a few minutes, so he stopped preaching, turned to his prayer team and told them to get down on their knees and shift that cloud! They did so, and when the time came to invite people to turn to Christ, over 5,000 came forward, many of them screaming and writhing with demons. A good time to have a prayer team on board!

Such a confidence doesn't come overnight – he recalls an incident which happened years ago which proved to be a major turning point in his prayer life.

'It was during the beginning stages of my ministry.

Nicky Cruz

I was in a very run-down motel, just a bed in a very small room. Here in this room, I had one of the most significant experiences of my life. As I began to pray and seek God, something extraordinary happened to me. I began to sense a great intimacy with God. A closeness that transcended all physical presence, a closeness, an intimacy in which no secrets existed. I began to weep, breaking down before God as I recognized his mighty presence . . . I recognized that I was nothing, and that he was everything, that I was totally dependent upon him. With loud sobbing, I told him that I loved him, that he was my Lord, my King, my Strength, my Power, and that without him, I was nothing – and then he touched me – and I discovered the true secret of how to become what God wants me to become. The secret was not to fast more, to read the Bible more, to go to church more or get formal education. No, the secret was intimacy with my God'.

Intimacy requires creativity, and predictably, the Latin American Nicky hates predictability! Unlike his beautiful wife Gloria, whom he admires because she 'gets up early every morning to pray and read', or his old friend Dave Wilkerson ('he's not always easy to get along with, but he prays beautifully'), Nicky is a man who tends to shy away from fixed patterns or rigid disciplines. 'I've learned not to be so hard on myself, not to be so legalistic', he admits with a wry smile, remembering that in the early days his spiritual intensity sometimes led him to live an unbalanced life – he fasted once and lost nine pounds and tottered close to a nervous breakdown in the process! The seasoned man seems more at peace with himself and God, freer, more spontaneous. He refuses to keep a journal of prayer and study. 'I hate them. I don't want to focus on

Friends of God

history, on the past. I want to go for the future'.

Now he tends to take a more all-round approach to his friendship with Jesus, 'I feel like one of those guys who carried the Ark of the Lord upon his shoulder: his presence is everywhere with me'. He also is in the habit of taking frequent 'five-minute mental vacations' when he just stops for a while, reads, thinks, prays, listens. 'His voice is inside my heart – I have never heard God speak to me audibly, but sometimes that inner voice sounds like thunder'. At other times he will find himself being drawn into deep intercession with 'lots of moaning and groaning – God will grab me, and I have to really empty myself before him, particularly before going through a valley experience'.

Intimacy also means honesty and reality with God. 'He knows me anyway, and he loves me regardless of who or what I am'.

Sometimes 'spirituality' breeds pious intolerance, but Cruz is patient with weakness, but wary of the false perfection and pretence of the 'big name personality gurus' who dominate the American evangelical sub-culture: 'The American Church has lost its virginity, it's consumed with gimmicks which some of our leaders, like witch doctors, are happy to provide. So many people in the ministry are in terrible shape these days. You find them full of "love" on the outside, particularly when the TV cameras are focused in. But inside, they are actors – hustlers playing the angles of their own imaginary religious game show – saying all the right things at the right times'. His voice is sharp with anger, and as he pounds his desk, I am glad to see a glimpse of the street fighter (sanctified!) again. Billy Graham is one of the 'big-time' evangelists whom Nicky has found worthy of consistent respect, but it was the quiet confidence of a professor during bible school days that most influenced Nicky in his own prayer life. 'I could respect him because he made mistakes, he was far from perfect, but he loved God with all his heart'. He believes that many of the scandals and mistakes could be avoided if trans-local ministry was firmly rooted in local church: 'I belong to a fine congregation (Radiant Church in Colorado Springs), where I learn new things constantly, fellowship with folk without whom my life would be empty. We evangelists get into trouble when we are not under anyone's authority: I placed myself under submission to my pastor, Don Steiger, and I'm grateful for his frequent input into my life . . .'

Nicky is a very practical man, who doesn't spend hours praying over every one of the many invitations that come in from all over the world: 'I take what comes in as an open door from God!' He doesn't see too many dreams and visions, but when they come, they're powerful, for example, when one of his colleagues was murdered: 'God gave me a vision and I saw one of our Teen Challenge guys being killed: I saw where it happened, who did it – everything. God showed it all to me'.

Impressive stuff. But does this apparently mighty man of God ever experience doubt, or get depressed? That smile came again: 'I'm glad that you asked that question. Yes, I do get depressed sometimes, particularly after coming home from an intensive time of ministry. One time I went to South America and had an amazing series of meetings. I felt like I was walking through the book of Acts, such miracles were happening. I was scheduled to appear on national television for two minutes and they extended the time to twenty-one minutes! The crowds were huge, so big that, when the crusade

Friends of God

team went shopping, they closed the shopping centre down completely so that we would be able to buy things without being interrupted! One of the leading lights in the Latin entertainment industry got saved: amazing things were happening, God felt so close. And then I came home, and stayed in the basement for two days, depressed and crying. Gloria came down, and called to me, "Where are you Nicky – what's going on?" I felt like I wanted to die . . .'

As I listened to Nicky, I remembered Elijah who beat the prophets of Baal on Mount Carmel and from there went straight to Mount Sinai to pray for death – post-ministry blues of the darkest sort . . .

Nicky continued: 'Yes, I have doubts sometimes, but doubts are beautiful, in that they are a call to faith, to go deeper, to pursue God more. Doubts don't move God – he's still there'. I was relieved: the hero has his bad days too!

Nickly loves scriptures, but again, he doesn't tend to follow a bible study timetable, preferring instead to study themes of interest throughout scripture. 'Look over there', he pointed to a bulging filing cabinet: 'Hundreds of sermons that I have never preached, and never will – but I needed to study – just for me'. He names Paul's letter (another ex-criminal and jailbird!) to the Philippians as his favourite book.

So how can we, as Paul wrote in that letter, 'Press on towards the goal . . . (which is) in Christ Jesus' (Phil. 3:14)? Nicky had some advice for those who are seeking to be faithful to God like he is – for life.

'Take a break of a day or two every three months, and be honest with God, especially about your sins. But don't be too hard on yourself – and don't try to do too much. If you can only eat one hamburger, don't try and eat two – you'll get constipated!

Nicky Cruz

Accept God's chastisement gladly – he does that because he loves you. Get back on track when you get off'.

He has obviously come a long way since the old New York street gang days, but this honest, fiery, lovable man is on the journey with God still. The street fighter (retired) now sends me away from his office with a warm hug and an armload of his best-selling books . . . and a powerful word to remember:

'Remember that God will never forget you, never leave you in a dark alley'.

Christine Noble

The discipline of grace

Christine Noble is a well-known speaker both in the UK and abroad. She is a member of the Pioneer Team network of churches and author of numerous books. She is a mother of five and a grandmother of ten.

Christine Noble was sitting in bed one night, reading. Suddenly she gasped – and tossed the book at the ceiling.

'This is dreadful,' she exclaimed to her husband John, sitting beside her.

Christine's spontaneous action says a great deal about her character. She has been pioneering to see women enabled to play an equal role to men in church life on and off for more than thirty years now. And she's still going strong, strong being a word that's often been used to describe her, both by those paying her a compliment – and those who aren't!

She chuckles mischievously when recalling the book-hurling incident. 'I tend to throw all books at the ceiling if I don't agree with them! There are probably quite a few dents up there by now!'

Although this home-loving 55-year-old grandma who collects stamps (with trees on them!) in her spare time doesn't like being described as a pioneer among women – 'far too religious' – there's no doubt that this is what she is. Her impact on the church over the past three decades has been considerable.

But like all innovative works, it started small and at home. The woman's place? Well, in the early 1960s, yes, it was.

Neither Christine nor John were Christians when they got married. Quite the opposite: they dabbled in the occult, and like many who play the devil's games, they soon found out that there was a dark and dangerous side to it all.

Friends of God

'That made us realize that there must be a good side to the supernatural, as well,' said Christine in her home in Romford, Essex.

'We decided to investigate. We started reading our bibles. I can't say that I've ever had a "conversion" experience. I just decided to give God a whirl and reckoned that if he was real, I'd soon find out! You could say that I've been giving him a whirl ever since!'

John and Christine ended up attending the Salvation Army where John had several profound encounters with God before they both got baptized in the Holy Spirit. But although John went on with God in leaps and bounds, the new power-packed Christine sadly became disillusioned with church because of its attitude towards women. So she stayed at home and busied herself with her children.

'I only went to church when I had to and I would wear the biggest hat that I could find, just to show I was conforming!' she said with a twinkle in her eye.

Little did she know that her 'home alone' decision marked the start of a highly significant work that God was going to do through her.

She said: 'Up until then I had discovered that God seemed to have a preference for men and didn't like extrovert actresses like me who wore red nail varnish. So I decided church wasn't for me. I simply asked God to use me where I was'.

To say that God answered that prayer would be an understatement! The home became a focal point. Neighbours, friends and young people, some from John's bible class, were always popping in. Many became Christians, were healed of physical and emotional problems, filled with the Holy Spirit and released from the grip of evil spirits. An entire

Christine Noble

Methodist youth group was turned upside down when many were baptized in the Holy Spirit! There was always something happening and John used to come home from church meetings to find out what God had been doing while he'd been out! It seemed that God had started a house church, but no-one realized it or accepted that it was possible – after all, women simply don't start churches, do they?

God later started speaking to John about creating a working model of a church in the home, and so he began 'regular' meetings in their front room – or was it that he joined in what God was doing there already?

Whichever it was, his decision threw up a new dilemma for Christine. For now that God's activity in her home had been formally recognized as a church, that meant that she had to start wearing a head covering – and most certainly *couldn't* take a leading role. So she stepped back.

She said: 'At that point I genuinely believed this was the right thing to do. I'd never been taught any different. When you look back on it, it just shows how ridiculous some theology is! I could be myself in my own home and see God use me to help people, get them saved and taught and healed and that was fine. But as soon as we called what was going on a 'church', I had to put on a hat and function differently in the meetings! Isn't that crazy? But that's the way we understood things then'.

The result was confusion. Christine went into hibernation again and stopped using the gifts of the Holy Spirit altogether.

The crunch point came when elders were appointed. Christine wasn't one of them – despite the fact that she had been shouldering as much eldership-type responsibility as the men. She was

Friends of God

bitterly disappointed and very hurt. 'I wanted to know what everyone else was doing that I wasn't doing. In the end it all boiled down to the fact that I was a woman and they weren't. And although John was totally against women in eldership in those days, he was wrestling with the subject'.

Christine was in a lonely place. She felt frustrated because she couldn't function in the ways she had done in the past. She felt torn between her understanding of theology on the one hand and her own contrary gut instincts on the other. John and Christine went through some extremely difficult times together.

'I felt utterly alone. It was just me and God – as it had been so many times before,' she recalled.

Fortunately, God did what he often does and used this painful, wilderness time to give birth to a new revelation.

Christine started studying scripture to find out what God really *did* say about women. She started, like Julie Andrews, at the very beginning – in Genesis. And gradually God revealed to her a truth that was the foundation of everything that Christine has done among women ever since. He showed her that the woman *wasn't* an after-thought in the creation process as she had previously been told.

She explained: 'Up until then I'd genuinely thought that God created man in his own image and that therefore man alone was really made in God's image. But suddenly I realized that if Adam was really made in God's image and Eve was taken out of him, then she too must be as full of God's being as he was. In fact one without the other is an incomplete representation of the Father. That made all the difference in the world to me'.

This revelation also changed the way Christine

Christine Noble

saw herself. She realized that she wasn't someone who was an afterthought. She was equal with men in God's sight! And like all of God's revelations, it brought about a change in the way she lived. Gradually she came out of her self-imposed shell and did more in the new church, now called Collier Row Christian Fellowship. Bringing up five children obviously occupied most of her time, but she began to take on more and more responsibilities and was eventually given the delightful title of 'Mother in Israel'.

Christine laughed: 'Being a Mother in Israel means that you carry out all kinds of leadership functions but cannot be called a leader because you're a woman! Isn't it all absurd! And you'll never believe the problems that arose when this Mother in Israel started giving birth to spiritual sons as well as spiritual daughters!'

Eventually John and his other leaders at Collier Row underwent a major theological shift and recognized women overseers – with Christine being the first. And she started to realize that she was just one of a number of women whom God had been shaping in the same way. She started meeting people like Faith Forster and Jean Darnell and was really encouraged that they'd been going through similar experiences. She wasn't alone any more.

The rest is history now – many churches changed their stances and enabled women to fulfil their role in all the main ministries, including leadership. And although the issue is clearly still a contentious one, Christine relishes the fact that she is now functioning in a senior leadership ministry, looking after several churches. Whatever next!

Criticism still dogs her, though. She is still called a 'strong woman' and says: 'Now, when people say

Friends of God

that to me I always treat it as a compliment, even if it isn't meant as one. But it used to be very painful at times, because the implication was that a strong woman can't be feminine in the traditionally accepted way. That was a bit rich, because I love cooking and ironing and doing things around the house and I often knit my own designs! The 'Proverbs 31' woman seems to be a good all-rounder! I've never seen a contradiction between being a housewife and a church leader. I love both. But it does seem to cause other people some problems.

'People calling me strong made it very difficult for me to understand and accept how God had made me. For either my personality had to undergo a major change, or God had made a major mistake in making me the way that he did. It was a very confusing time'.

Although the church has made enormous strides since those early days in recognizing that women can exercise biblical gifts, Christine still does not believe that the work is done yet. She still reckons that women find it hard to believe that God speaks to them because they have been taught that there is something about them that makes them vulnerable to deception.

'There is a lot of pain inside many, many women,' Christine said. 'The enemy has inflicted enormous damage upon us. Satan is still saying to women what he said to Eve in the Garden of Eden, "Did God really say that?" He knows our susceptibility to doubt.

'Many women are deeply affected by tremendous doubts about their gifts and ministries and need to be released from those fears. People still think it was all Eve's fault in the Garden of Eden. They forget

Christine Noble

that Adam just sat there and let it all happen. Women need to be broken out of this doubt syndrome. At the moment some women are at the stage where they know that, theologically, there is nothing to stop them functioning. But emotionally they still aren't able to. They don't need any more training or equipping. They simply need releasing into what God has for them – and freeing from the emotional doubts and fears that stop them'.

With this in mind, Christine is currently organizing a series of conferences called 'Into Focus' through the Pioneer network of churches and beyond. She hopes to see a major breakthrough in the way women function in church life.

The word 'revelation' plays a big part in Christine's conversation. She is the kind of person who sees things from God quite regularly. But how do these revelations actually come?

It's all very normal. Christine is a 'picture' person and will often see a picture in her mind while she is driving to Sainsburys, doing the washing up or sitting in her rocking chair. One such picture cured her from terrible panic attacks that used to afflict her. Others have helped people in counselling or when Christine's been helping out in churches.

The revelations come, though, out of a lifestyle that is thoroughly immersed in prayer and bible study.

Her prayer life, predictably, is very spontaneous. Christine prays a lot, especially while she is on the move – a habit which grew out of necessity when she was looking after five children *and* doing some child minding at the same time. It has served her well since. And she often prays in tongues, especially when she doesn't know what else to pray.

However, Christine realizes that spontaneity and

Friends of God

the whole area of revelation can be unreliable, so she is careful to do plenty of bible study to use as a foundation. She studies in different ways at different times. She is currently reading the Bible through in a year, but because she's a very fast reader, she is in fact reading it through *three* times in a year instead. She studies chunks from the Old Testament, New Testament and Psalms/Proverbs each day. 'Jeremiah's one long moan!' she chuckled. 'He's really hard work! My favourite Old Testment books are Ezra, Nehemiah and Esther, and I tend to want to linger over them for longer. But it's all God's word – and all this intensive reading provides the fuel which God can use to ignite with the fire of revelation'.

Although discipline does not play a major part in her spontaneous spiritual lifestyle, there is one area where she is very strict. An unusual area. She says: 'Enjoying and accepting God's forgiveness is a more important discipline in a Christian's life than prayer or bible study. When we do wrong we feel we have to feel sorry for ourselves for ages and we stew in our own juice. This cuts us off from God and then prayer and bible study stop straight away. We need to be disciplined in confessing our sins – and as equally disciplined in forgetting about them afterwards, in the same way as God does. I'm sure this is the key to a more Godly life'.

Christine is no stranger to miracles. She has seen them when she has prayed for other people, and has seen them in her own life, too. She still speaks with amazement about the time when God multiplied money in her purse during a time of real hardship. She was out shopping, and every time she went into a shop and bought something, she still had 50p left in loose change!

Christine Noble

She said: 'It really was quite remarkable! There was no doubt that it was God. We were so poor in those days I had to be meticulous with my change, so it certainly wasn't a question of my miscounting the money. I took a deep breath and went to as many shops as possible – I even collected some things from the cleaners and some shoes from the menders. They were both items we hadn't been able to afford! And not only did I have enough to pay for them – but I actually had some money left in my purse afterwards'.

Christine has been active in Christian work for several decades now and she's still going strong with God – and loving every minute of it. Her heart remains full of vision for the future – full of new prospects and new challenges.

She currently feels God is speaking to her about systematic fasting as preparation for encounters with the demonic realm.

She expects to spend the next two or three years helping women to break through the emotional pain barriers and into effective ministry, and is looking forward to the possibility of going to Singapore in 1994 – a country which she has been concerned about for a number of years.

She is also keen to put her acting experience to good effect. She is a trained actress, and is eager to draw alongside people who work in the arts and give them encouragement and support. And she has a feeling that God may be calling her to do some work in the United States.

Despite all the excitement and the activity, working among churches, travelling, and writing, Christine is very honest about struggles in her relationship with God at the moment.

She said: 'He's a bit remote, and it is particularly

Friends of God

difficult praying to someone who seems cold and distant. That brings a conflict between what I feel and what I know about him. And yes, I do sometimes doubt that God exists, but not very strongly and not very regularly. Let's put it this way – I sometimes ask God if he exists! And he always tells me that he does!'

Whatever the struggles, Christine's zeal still burns strong. Her eyes still blaze with God's burdens. And so it's no surprise when she pauses, reflectively, and says: 'If I could choose what I'd like on my tombstone, it would be: "She heard from God . . . and lived dangerously" '.

Hopefully the day when the tombstone is needed is a long way off. But there's no doubt that the epitaph is being lived out in reality already.

Clive Calver

A heart for the nation

Clive Calver is General Director of the Evangelical Alliance, President of the Crusaders and Vice President of the Universities and Colleges Christian Fellowship and of British Youth for Christ.

A van skids in a busy London street and crashes into some parked cars.

In a large, book-lined office nearby, Clive Calver is describing how his life tends to skid from one crisis to another – with a few crashes along the way.

The leader of Britain's Evangelical Alliance hears the prang outside and leaps from his desk to see what's happened. 'Some of our staff have cars parked out there,' he exclaimed. 'I hope there isn't any damage'.

There isn't. But it seems rather appropriate that the crash happened while Clive was talking about coping with life's storms. For trouble never seems far away from the 42-year-old father of four. It seems that he read Jesus' warning that 'in this life you will have trouble' and decided to apply it with as much enthusiasm as possible. He loves living on the knife-edge.

Take, for instance, one summer's day in the Calver family a while ago.

At 6 a.m. a burglar kicked in the front door of his large semi-detached house in a south London cul-de-sac and stole a handbag belonging to his wife Ruth. It contained all her holiday money.

Later the same day, his 13-year-old son Kris was threatened at knifepoint and had his beloved mountain bike stolen. He'd saved all his money specially to buy it.

Then a few hours after that Ruth was indoors again, recovering from the dawn visit by the burglar, when she was shot at by an enthusiast with an air gun. The would-be Young Gun blew out one of the windows of the family home.

Recalled Clive: 'Ruth turned to me and said: "Well, we must be doing something right!" After all, it's not every day that a family gets burgled, mugged and shot at in the space of twelve hours!'

So how did the Calvers cope with this extraordinary series of events which might have made even Job drop him a sympathy card? Clive smiled the famous smile which has become so familiar on platforms across the country and said: 'Well, we didn't rebuke the devil fifteen times. We prayed together! What else could you do? I've found that if I live with life's struggles, I become a better guy. I'm not denying that the devil sometimes attacks us. But we need to see that sometimes it is God who rocks our boat, not the devil. God uses him to refine our characters'.

Clive is certainly used to coping with life's storms. In fact he seems to specialize in it. Once he hit black ice while driving his car and was heading fast for another vehicle coming in the opposite direction.

'I prayed all the way until I hit it!' he laughed. 'I had a hitch-hiker on board at the time. I'm not sure what surprised him most – the crash or the prayer! The two cars collided head on and mine was written off. But we both walked out unhurt.

'The hitch-hiker ran for his life! But that's what my life's like – living from one crisis to another and meeting God along the way'.

Clive's relaxed, flexible approach to this turbulent lifestyle is reflected in his equally relaxed and flexible prayer life.

He reached for a cup of black coffee in his office at the headquarters of the Evangelical Alliance in London and uttered the words which could incite

Friends of God

a riot among some Christians: 'I don't have a quiet time,' he said. 'There simply isn't enough time in the day. I often have to be up at 6 a.m. to get to work for a meeting. It just wouldn't be practical.

'If I was the pastor of a church, it would be different. I'd allocate an hour a day to pray. But my days simply don't work like that'.

So what *does* he do?

'Discipline *is* important. I can't be effective in my job if I'm not hearing from God. So I take time to pray at various times of the day – sometimes five or six times. Sometimes I pray on my own, but most of the time it's with others. I pray every night with my wife Ruth.

'When I pray on my own I tend to pray very quietly – I'm a very private person. And I don't like being interrupted,' he added in a serious tone that dared anyone to try it.

Clive added: 'I'm nothing if God isn't with me. There's no human reason why you'd expect that he would be with me. But he is. He's there correcting me, helping me, telling me where I'm wrong. He's always there.

'One of my most frequent prayers is "Help Lord". I mean, if you were about to do a live news broadcast, or take part in a discussion on the radio with the chief witch, what would *you* pray? Unless God's there in situations like these, I'm dead. That might sound dramatic, but it's true.

'After all, who on earth am I to be discussing major religious issues with people like Ludovic Kennedy? I'm just a kid off the streets of East London. I sometimes scratch my head and wonder what I'm doing in these high-power situations. But God never lets me down'.

It is this fast-lane existence as General Director

Clive Calver

of the EA that has led Clive to have an unshakeable faith in God. But surely he sometimes doubts that God is really there – or gets fed up talking to someone he can't see?

'Never,' he said. 'No, never. God's presence is close to me all the time. His presence is so immanent. He's proved it to me unfailingly, time and time again. How could I possibly doubt him?'

What about when he's sick? Surely, everyone doubts God's promises when they're sick, and then pray and discover nothing happens. Once again, Clive Calver is humorously philosophical. 'When I'm sick, I get better!' he said. 'It doesn't really matter how. I call for the elders to pray for me. If it works, I go back to work. If it doesn't I go to bed and catch up on some reading until I am better. If necessary, I'll call the doctor. Whatever happens, I end up recovering, and that's what matters'.

And what does God's voice sound like to Clive? He thought carefully, and said: 'I have heard God speak strongly on rare occasions and I have heard him speak gently quite often'.

Clive is very honest with God. And he finds that God is very honest with him. Clive tells him everything – and sometimes vents his anger. Although he is warm and friendly, and has a great sense of humour, he is also a man of principle. His friendly manner belies a man who gets angry with hypocrisy, spiritual naïveté, injustice, commercialism and self-righteousness. But this is all tempered with a strong degree of trust that God knows what he's doing in situations where Clive gets cross.

And does Clive see pictures, dreams and visions when he prays?

He said: 'Pictures don't often enter my prayer life.

Friends of God

I don't like them – I've got too vivid an imagination. I think I might get carried away! But I do experience very strong leanings in the word of wisdom and sometimes get clear prophetic words.

'As for dreams, yes, I do sometimes get them – especially about four months before Spring Harvest! And they can easily turn into nightmares! I'm a very sound sleeper – I could sleep through Armageddon and not realize it had happened. So God doesn't even try to wake me in the night to talk to me like he does some people. But he does sometimes chuck something into my last dream of the night so that I can still remember it in the morning. However, that only happens around three or four times a year'.

His job as General Director of the EA means that he's the spearhead of an umbrella organization that represents a million churchgoers from more than twenty denominational streams.

He has written five books and was co-founder of Spring Harvest, which is now one of the world's largest worship and teaching events. You'll regularly see him on television, hear him on the radio and see his name in the papers.

It is easy to put high-profile people like Clive on a pedestal. After all, that's where most people see him – on a stage. There can be few evangelical Christians who haven't heard him speak and been impressed with his passion and his vision. But do men like him ever make mistakes?

He laughed. 'If I was infallible I'd apply for a job in Rome! Once I gave a prophetic word in a meeting and as I finished I saw a good friend of mine shaking his head. He told me later "The first two lines were the Lord. The rest was you".

'But that's what it's all about, isn't it – learning as you go – being prepared to make mistakes. That

Clive Calver

means that you're making yourself vulnerable. And that's healthy. I make mistakes and I've never met anyone who doesn't. In fact I get really worried if I hear someone say that they don't make mistakes. That's just not natural. But having said that, I tend to know my weak areas and I cover myself'.

Quietly-spoken Clive describes himself as a mercurial character, which is why it is hard to put his prayer life into any kind of pigeon-hole. It is as flexible as he is. The same goes for using the gift of tongues and fasting. He uses both when he needs to – but not in a regular, disciplined way.

He said: 'If you said to me "My wife's dying of cancer. Would you be prepared to fast for her?", then I probably would. But I don't fast every week on a given day or anything like that.

'And I only use tongues when I find it hard to articulate to God what I mean in English. I drive my spiritual father, Alec Buchanan, to despair. He's intensely disciplined, but to his credit he's never tried to make me behave like him. He's a firm believer in allowing people to be different'.

However, Clive does not use this flexible, spasmodic approach in all aspects of his walk with God. That would be far too straightforward! He's intensely disciplined with his bible study.

He aims to read the Bible right through once a year and keeps a chart to show whether he's up or down on schedule. He splits the Bible up into four roughly equal portions and reads a chapter from each every day.

He said: 'I've got a degree in theology and I've been recovering ever since. That's why I do plenty of bible study! But I find it's important to be disciplined. You can stop for a moment and pray. You can stop for a moment and speak in tongues.

Friends of God

You can stop for a moment and decide to fast. But you can't stop for a moment and study the Bible. You need to give it time. And that's what I do. I spend a lot of time reading the Bible'.

Despite having a busy schedule, Clive still has time for the occasional round of golf and for cooking Italian, Indian and Chinese food. And then there are his children and his Dalmatian, Tozer – the third Calver hound to bear the illustrious name of the great Christian author.

His children are his hobby. He takes them to all kinds of places together and they do all kinds of crazy things. And they always come first. One day Clive had promised to take his daughter to the zoo. Then the BBC rang and asked him to do a spot on *World at One*. He said that he would do it on the way to the zoo – or not at all. He wasn't prepared to let his girl down.

Clive's openness and obedience to God were really challenged two years ago when he had to make some decisions about his future.

It was suggested that he apply for another significant job – not just once, but several times. It was a difficult time, but one in which God confirmed Clive's calling in a most dramatic way.

In December 1990 he believed God told him that Paul Cain, an American with a remarkable prophetic ministry, had a word from God for him.

He apprehensively told his executive at the EA about it and they gave him the go-ahead to find Paul Cain in America. Clive was preparing to enjoy a trip to the States, but Paul turned up in England, ministering at Holy Trinity Church, Brompton, just a few miles away from Clive's office!

Clive went along to a meeting there and sat right at the back with his friend Gerald Coates, director of the Pioneer Trust. Words of knowledge and prophecies came and went – but there was nothing for Clive.

He recalled: 'I was convinced Paul had something for me. And I was right! It was the last word he gave. He said that he had a word for someone named C-A-L-V-E-R – he spelt my name out.

'Then he went on to repeat word for word my original calling which came in a prophetic word given to me a number of years ago. I was bowled over'.

That original word came in the form of a picture – of a blade of corn lying on a path. On one side there was a field, ready for harvest. On the other side was a field that was bare. God's call to Clive was not to be in either field, but in the middle, taking food from the plentiful field to help the one that was bare.

That night at Holy Trinity, Paul Cain confirmed that word completely. He said Clive stood between the prophetic and non-prophetic sides of the church and had a role in bringing them together. That is what he has been doing for many years now – and Paul's word was God's call to continue.

Said Clive: 'Paul had never met me nor heard of me. I was dumbfounded. But it's that kind of encounter with God that has made a big difference to me. And it suggested that I was to stay where I was, with the EA'. Later, in the quietness of personal meditation, gazing across the Sea of Galilee, the Lord used the pages of scripture to confirm the point.

And where is Clive's walk with God at the moment? He paused and said: 'It's in process – and hopefully getting better every year. By getting better, I mean that I'm realizing more and more that I'm

Friends of God

forgiven, and I'm spending more time with God and less time on work.

'I used to serve God to earn his favour. But we all need to serve him because we love him, and learn to love him even if we don't serve him at all.

'I'm still learning that. It's a process. And one that will never end'.

Margaret Cundiff

Straight talk, with love

Writer and broadcaster Margaret Cundiff is Parish Deacon at St James' Church, Selby, North Yorkshire and Broadcasting Officer for the York Diocese.

It's the morning service in a small Anglican church in Selby, a busy Yorkshire market town. Halfway back, a woman in her late thirties is sitting in a pew, struggling to concentrate on the sermon.

Her mind wanders. How's the Sunday roast doing? What shall we do with the children this afternoon? The sermon rambles on.

Suddenly the woman hears a voice from behind her.

'Be filled with the Spirit!'

Startled, the woman looks round. Behind her, a row of people are sitting listening – perhaps – to the sermon. Clearly, none of them have spoken. The voice continues. 'Be filled with the Spirit!' And again. 'Be filled with the Spirit!'

Eventually the sermon comes to an end, but the voice continues. The woman goes up to receive Holy Communion, hoping that the voice will go away. Still it continues and she realizes that this isn't any old voice. This is the voice of God. Eventually Margaret Cundiff gives in. 'Lord,' she says, while kneeling at the communion rail, 'I don't understand this at all, but whatever it is, Yes.' Peace and freedom flood her being.

Twenty-three years later, Margaret, now sixty-one, still remembers that encounter with God clearly. And she's emphatic: 'Yes it *was* an audible voice, not just something in my imagination. I heard it with my ears – that's why I looked round to see who had spoken. And when it continued I couldn't understand why nobody else had heard it.

Margaret Cundiff

Eventually, I realized it was only me who could hear it – and who it was who was speaking. I was quite frightened!

'There was no doubt that it was God. It's never really happened since, or at least, not as clearly as that. But there have certainly been other times when I have had to respond to some very positive promptings by God'.

It is obvious after hearing this story that Margaret is no ordinary go-to-church-on-Sunday Anglican. She's a mischievous tough-talking, charismatic ('with a small "c" please'), a deacon who is happy to stay within a traditional denomination but who is far more radical in her thinking than many people who have joined newer churches, rejecting the older ones as 'religious'!

And since that life-changing encounter with God back in the 1970s Margaret's ministry has grown enormously: she now writes books, makes regular broadcasts both locally and nationally and is especially well known for her contributions to BBC Radio's *Pause for Thought*.

As well as being Broadcasting Officer for the York Diocese, she currently serves in St James', a small family church in Selby. There, her practical care and down-to-earth approach to life have endeared her to a population which has caught the rough end of the recession.

Margaret has been involved in Anglican churches almost all her life, and as a result, brings a refreshing perspective on Church of England traditions and practices.

She said: 'I'm not at all keen on some of this modern-day worship, where everyone's so matey with God. I know he's our friend, but very often these days people lose their sense of awe and respect

Friends of God

for him. I mean, you wouldn't breeze up to the Queen or the Archbishop and start being all pally, would you? And yet this is how people treat God.

'In the Bible, Isaiah fell before God in awe. That's what we should do sometimes. And being swept into a stranger's arms during the middle of a service is not my idea of worship. So many songs these days are full of words about ourselves. They don't focus on God.

'Music is a language to God – and God sees no difference between older music and the newer stuff, providing your heart's right. To me, listening to a sung evensong in a cathedral is like a touch of heaven. It's beautiful – and God speaks through it, if you let him. The old songs often contain words to express deep things to God which simply don't exist in new ones.

'And I'm a firm believer in having a set order of service – a structure. People love to feel secure and know what's coming next, so they can relax and enjoy God's presence. But having said that, we all need to be sensitive to one another and realize that it takes all sorts to make a world. I'd never criticize people who do things differently'.

How does Margaret respond to criticisms of Anglican traditions, robes and buildings? She's one of the most non-religious people you'll ever meet – but has no problem with the 'religiosities'.

Margaret wears robes – and is proud to do so. She said: 'There's a real freedom in wearing clerical garb, especially for me as a woman. If I stood in the pulpit to preach wearing a dress, people would say "Oh, I don't like the colour of that," or "She wore that the other week!" That would stop them from listening. But if I wear my robes, they concentrate on what I'm saying, not on me.

Margaret Cundiff

'As for old Anglican buildings, yes, we all know that the church is people, not buildings. But if you go in some of these old churches, you'll find a presence of God which you simply don't discover in newer ones. Just think – they've been prayed in for centuries, some of them. That makes a difference'.

Margaret's love of time-honoured Anglican traditions affects her personal relationship with God in a very deep way. She studies the Bible keenly, but follows the set Church of England readings, both in her private devotions and her preaching. Again, this disciplined approach is often criticized – but she has found positive benefits.

She explained: 'I find that by following the set readings, you cover the whole of the Bible, not just parts of it. It's surprising how many people only read certain parts of scripture – most groups and denominations have their favourite bits. And there's always a danger with finding passages that fit what you want to hear and which don't make you too uncomfortable. Set readings give you an all-round theology. The Bible's like a stick of rock – wherever you break it, it's got "Jesus" all the way through.

'Those of us who are ministers need to be careful in the way we read the Bible. So often I open the book and as I begin to read, I'm already working out an introduction and three points for a talk. Doing that has been described somewhere as "the rape of the word". That sounds strong stuff, but it's true. So often we come to the Bible simply to take out what we want. We find it hard to sit down with the Bible, open it and let it speak to us, for no other reason than that it is the word of God. At times when I sit down and read it through for the sheer love of

Friends of God

it and out of a desire to hear God speak, then I'm rewarded'.

Margaret is similarly structured in her prayer life. She makes appointments with God – and enters them in her diary! And he's never missed one – or been late!

The practice started when she discovered that her diary was always full of appointments with all kinds of people – everyone, in fact, other than the person whom she loves more than anyone.

And she's quite honest in admitting that despite being one of the people who can claim they've heard God speak to them audibly, she still finds prayer a battle.

She said: 'It's this dreadful time business, isn't it? There are always other things you could be doing, and so we give God the dregs of our time; either that, or we only pray when we need an "emergency service". We need to learn to wait on God – but none of us like waiting or queuing, do we? Very often I drive to the North Yorkshire Moors or to the coast and just sit and see his power and majesty, and enjoy his love for me. And every time I kick myself afterwards for not doing it more often.

'I try to link my prayer time to bible study or a Psalm. Scripture certainly is a help, and I find the Anglican prayer books are really valuable – they give you a place to start in your prayers'.

And how about the gift of tongues? 'No,' chuckles Margaret. 'I didn't speak in tongues when I received the Spirit that day. But there have often been occasions since when I use tongues when I pray – when I can't express myself in any other way. And when I pray for people, they often say "How did you know that?" Some people would say that was the gift of knowledge – and I'm sure that it is. But

Margaret Cundiff

I'm very wary about this term "charismatic". We are *all* filled with the Spirit. If I'm charismatic, then it's definitely with a small c!'

And this God whom Margaret heard that day – what is he like? How does Margaret see him? 'Over the years, different aspects of his character come over more strongly at different times. Put it this way. While I was at college, my tutor started off as a teacher, but as I got to know her better, she later became a counsellor, too. But then as the years went by, she became a friend. It's the same with God. At first, he was my guide, but now he's an old friend, in the best sense of the word. I'm comfortable with him, at ease with him. My relationship with him is built on experience and therefore I have no reason to doubt him'.

This relationship, as Margaret says, has been going a long time – since she was seventeen. That was when she was a firebrand, a teenage rebel, a lover of life. She went to an Anglican church in Mossley, and became a good friend of the vicar. But it took a straight talk from the famous Baptist minister Dr Alan Redpath at a British Youth for Christ meeting to stop her in her tracks. Up to then, she had assumed she was a Christian. But suddenly she realized there was a decision to make.

'That night I realized that being a Christian was about knowing Jesus – not just knowing about him or approving of what he'd done. And I met him – as one person meets another. And I knew that what he'd done, he'd done for me. It needed someone to lay it on the line – something that we don't do often enough with young people these days. We're happy to let them drift, without ever confronting them with the hard decisions they need to make'.

Margaret's closeness with God has been greatly

Friends of God

tested in recent years by two issues – the recession and the controversy over women priests.

The recession has ravaged her community in Selby, a pretty little market town around fifteen miles from York and Leeds, surrounded by little villages – and power stations.

Selby coal field is the most modern in Europe, but when it opened, it inflicted massive change on the community. The local churches played a major role in preparing the community for the transition – but since then other pit closures have left their mark. Unemployment has bitten deep. Families and communities have broken up as people have travelled elsewhere to find work.

Margaret explained: 'A lot of older people have no family living nearby any more. It's terrible for them. Whereas up to now their children and grandchildren have all lived nearby because they worked nearby, now they've gone. So we as a church try to be a family to them, offering as much care and love and practical support as we can. But it's not been easy – and it still isn't'.

Not surprisingly, Margaret has been right in the thick of the row over the ordination of women – and there are no prizes in guessing which side she has been on! She was a deaconess for ten years until the Church of England Synod voted for women deacons, and was one of the first to be ordained deacon in York Minster in 1987 following that vote. She has frequently appeared on television to argue the case of women, and is looking forward to becoming a priest one day – if her church decides to accept her!

Her uncomplicated nature often finds it hard to understand what all the fuss is about. And of course, she is delighted that the Church of England Synod

Margaret Cundiff

– where she served for five years – has now given the go-ahead for women to be ordained.

But she said: 'I suppose there will still be a lot of heartache, and people are going to be hurt on both sides. Relationships will be affected in many ways. It's inevitable, really.

'It will only be as we see each other as brother and sister, as we love each other as we are, with all our fears and hang-ups, with all our vulnerability, and are able to say "Jesus died for *us*" that we will be able, by the grace of God, to face the future together'.

Margaret has received her fair share of stick as the debate has raged – and still sees red when members of the anti-women lobby talk about women becoming 'priestesses' – with the implications of witchcraft all too clear to see.

But fortunately, her impish sense of humour has helped her keep things in perspective – and helped to maintain most of her relationships with those who don't see things the way she does.

She said: 'God and I have a lot of fun together. Woody Allen once said "If you want to make God laugh, tell him your future plans". I think he was right. God's got a wonderful sense of humour – the Bible is full of fun. Jesus made loads of throw-away lines which I'm sure he intended to be funny and nothing else. Yet people have seized on them and tried to form deep theological statements around them. How sad. Humour cuts us down to size – and we all need it. I've never been very good at humility!'

Margaret's not just funny. She's also tough and independent – characteristics which God has had to contend with on more than one occasion. She is not always easy to work with, doesn't like letting

Friends of God

people help her and loves to do things *her* way. But she knows her weaknesses and chuckles as she muses: 'I'm sure God says "I'll get her one day. I'll soften her up in her old age" '.

Margaret brings a refreshing simplicity and naturalness to Christianity which you don't often find these days. A few minutes chatting to her makes God seem much more real and problems far less difficult. In many ways, despite the fact that her ministry and sphere of influence have grown enormously, her lifestyle is the same as it's always been, with her husband Peter and grown-up son Julian – a well-known carp fisherman – living at their home near Selby. Their daughter, Alison, works for the Church Commissioners and lives in London but is often home to be with them and enjoy their family life together. Margaret is a firm believer in getting on with the ordinary things in life – and leaving the extraordinary things to God. It is hard to take in, when you are chatting to her, that you are listening to someone whose broadcasts are enjoyed by millions. But Margaret finds it hard to take in as well! She is constantly surprised at the ways God uses her – and by the fact that he uses her at all. 'Yes, I'm amazed at everything that's happened. You know, now I'm a Pastoral Selector – helping to select people who want to become ordained. And I often think "Well, if I had to interview someone like me, I definitely wouldn't select them!" But God chose me – it's a mystery why. And not only did he call me, but he's recalled me at times when I've failed. That says a lot about him, doesn't it?'

One of Margaret's favourite verses is the exclamation that Jacob made when he woke up from his dream at Bethel: 'Surely the LORD is in this place

Margaret Cundiff

and I was not aware of it' (Gn. 28:16). Margaret constantly finds that God turns up in the most unlikely places.

She says: 'I find him on trains, in the checkout at Safeways. I'm constantly going into strange places and new situations these days, but every time I find he's there, too. It's wonderful – and I'm always as surprised about it as Jacob was'.

Margaret, who describes herself as a bit proud, is in reality too humble to realize that very often, it is her faith and her close walk with God that enable her to recognize him in these situations. And one thing's for sure – there will be more situations like it. For if God uses the simple things to confound the wise, then he'll surely carry on using Margaret, with her simple, back-to-basics approach to life and faith, to reflect his heart across the nation.

Gerald Coates

A toast to life

Gerald Coates is one of the leaders of the New Church movement in Britain and head of his church 'Pioneer People'. He is also a frequent contributor to radio and television.

Gerald Coates. Mention the name in evangelical circles around the nation and you are guaranteed a reaction of some sort – he has been loved and loathed, quoted as a wise man and dismissed as a near heretic. Applauded as a 'colourful troubadour in a world of grey men' by one evangelical leader recently, he has carved a well-earned reputation as a man who refuses to accept the status quo, hates religiosity with a public passion, and has been responsible for the upsetting of a whole market full of apple carts.

Even the most cherished traditions have not escaped his piercing prophetic appraisal. Gerald has been very vocal through the years about the folly of 'devotional Christianity', loudly dismissing the notion that every Christian must have a daily 'quiet time' in order to walk with God. Not surprisingly, his outspoken lampooning of this broadly accepted idea has got him into serious hot water more than once! During one sermon when Gerald was slaughtering a few sacred cows in general and 'quiet times' in particular, a man stood up in the middle of the sermon and yelled out indignantly, 'You are a disgrace! You should be teaching these young people to get up every morning to pray and read their bibles – this is disgusting'. The meeting, understandably, went very quiet, until the heckler's wife piped up, and asked her loud husband 'Why do you say that? *You* never do it!' Gerald laughs when he recounts the story, but in many ways it sums up what he lives for – the debunking

Friends of God

of artificial, hypocritical unreality in the church.

It was, therefore, with great curiosity that I approached a meeting with Gerald Coates. I knew well enough what he was against in the realm of personal spirituality – but what was he *for*? He possesses a remarkable ability to communicate publicly, stirring and challenging and exhorting and annoying his audience all at the same time: but what is behind the public face of the man they call 'the gatherer'? (He seems to possess a real gift to draw Christians of widely diverging persuasions together, hence the name-tag.) What is the truth about Gerald and God?

I asked if there was *ever* a time when Gerald was conventional in the way he expressed his spirituality. 'Oh yes – and it was very unhelpful' he affirmed. 'Back in the early days of my faith I was persuaded by others that real "spiritual giants" got up at unheard of hours of the day to pray and read scripture. I genuinely wanted to please the Lord, so I did it – and it was dreadful. I was told that people like Wesley got up at 5.30 a.m., so I should too – and then I began to realize that we live in a completely different culture from that of Wesley – he went to bed when it got dark, and so was well able to get up at first light, whereas I rarely manage to conclude my day before midnight – so in a sense, if I can be up and in the office by 9 a.m., I may well be doing better than our forefathers!'

That's not to say that Gerald never sets time aside early in the morning to pray – there are occasions when he will specifically 'diary in' special early appointments with God, particularly if he finds himself involved in very important, strategic work. He almost got arrested during one of those early morning meetings with his Maker! 'I got up at 5.30 a.m. and went to Wisley Woods, a beautiful

Gerald Coates

spot near my home, and was walking through what I thought was a deserted area, singing and shouting and thanking God very loudly, my arms up in the air. Suddenly I noticed a white Rover car complete with red stripe and blue light, in which sat a large policeman with arms folded and a look of grave suspicion on his face!'

There are also times when Gerald will pray during the night. 'Sometimes I just wake up – I wouldn't go so far as to say, "The Lord woke me", but I feel awake and refreshed, and an ideal opportunity is presented to me to reflect, to read Scripture and allow it to wash over me . . .' This idea of the 'washing' effect of Scripture is one that he alludes to frequently. On one occasion he was part of an impressive group which gathered to debate religion and ethics for the Radio 4 programme *The Moral Maze*. One of the guests, who distributed gems during the broadcast such as 'It's all right to commit adultery as long as you don't hurt anyone', suddenly became somewhat animated, and accused Mr. Coates with a hiss (Gerald notes that atheists frequently hiss!), 'The trouble with you Christians is that you're all into brainwashing.'

Quickly came the reply: 'You know, that's a very astute observation. We Christians are into brainwashing – and so are you. The difference between us is that the stuff that we're washing our brains in is a jolly sight cleaner than the stuff you're washing your brains in!' That's not to suggest that Gerald is into the '1.75 chapters a day and a psalm' approach. 'I like to read a whole book through. That's the way they were designed to be read. Paul wrote a letter to the Ephesians, and therefore we should read it like a letter, not carve it up'.

So yes, the man does read the Bible – and pray. And there is often a structure to his praying. 'I

Friends of God

always begin any time with God by giving thanks. I thank him for everything that I can think of – colour, shape, the weather, friends, family, apricot brandy . . . I can't stand being around negative, ungrateful people who take every opportunity to complain.

'Then I spend some time acknowledging my failures. The Anglicans have a helpful approach, in that they confess the sins of omission and the sins of commission – asking God to forgive them for not doing what they ought to have done, and for doing that which they ought not to have done.

'Then I pray for family, friends, the church, the work of Pioneer, and those who are not yet Christians. God finds it hard to resist prayers prayed in the name of his Son!'

Gerald also spends time praying with his wife, Anona, though not every day. 'Our schedules don't allow for that. Anona works as a medical receptionist and so is often getting up at a different time from me – but we do pray together, probably a couple of times each week'.

With all this talk of prayer and bible study, you might be tempted to think that Gerald is veering towards a traditional devotional approach – and then he shares some of his other special times with God. 'Sometimes for me a time with God means going to a coffee shop in Esher with a copy of *Time* magazine or perhaps *Leadership Today* and sitting down and reading it through the eyes of Christ. Prophets are seers, which literally means that they see things, and there are times when I really see something of God's perspective in those moments'.

And he is scathing about the 'I'm going to have a me and my Jesus time' approach. 'The problem isn't having a personal relationship with Jesus, rather it's individualism that presents the difficulty. Much of our

Gerald Coates

devotion must be worked out together in our friendships – that's why the Bible pronounces the man who says he loves God but hates his brother to be a liar. The Bible says nothing about "Quiet" times, but much about being noisy and eating and drinking 'and just being together. The last thing we need in our individualistic society, where you live in a cube, go to work in a cube with wheels, and work in another cube, is more addiction to the individualistic. We are called to build community, to live our lives with Jesus and one another.' And fasting? 'I do fast when other members of the leadership team at Pioneer People, Cobham, are fasting, and I often miss meals because I'm giving myself to more important matters – but many Christians fast when in fact they've never really learned how to feast. Some of them don't like eating anyway! Christians need to learn the art of celebrating!'

His preparation for preaching is unusual as well – most of the time he finds himself driving to speaking engagements, so there is time alone in the car. 'I love to listen to Elton John, because Taupin's lyrics are so dynamic, and I find that the music prevents me from becoming "other worldly" in my own presentations. Or sometimes it's Handel, Mozart or Beethoven. I like to get to a meeting as late as possible, so as to avoid distractions, particularly if I'm nervous, which often happens if the meeting is very important – and importance has nothing to do with the size of the gathering'.

The more we talk, the more I become aware that Gerald Coates steadfastly refuses to divide his life into compartments, or practise what Richard Foster calls 'inner apartheid', where we 'segregate out a small corner of pious activities and then can make no sense of the rest of our lives – a five per cent spirituality'. Gerald considers that everything he does can be lived

Friends of God

in friendship and communion with God – in a sense, a literal 'prayer life', hence his little trips to shopping centres 'with the Lord'. As I listened to him talk, I was reminded of the words of Anthony Bloom: 'A prayer makes sense only if it is lived – unless life and prayer become completly interwoven, prayers become a sort of polite madrigal which you offer to God at moments when you are giving time to him'.

And the God who is his friend does seem to be very understanding about modern pressurised living. So speaks Gerald concerning one of his busier periods: 'I often go into the office and begin the day by saying "Good morning Lord". It's a way of affirming that I want to be doing his business today. One morning, as I spoke my customary greeting, I realized with great horror that I had not spent time in prayer for days – maybe even weeks – to be honest, I couldn't recall the time span. I felt so bad about this, that I immediately called out my apology to the Lord, asking him to forgive me for neglecting him. His reply staggered me, and I am certain that it was God speaking: "It's all right, Gerald, I know that you've been very busy!"

'I struggled with this, wondering if this could really be the voice of God – and then I realized that God is my Father. If one of my sons put his head round my study door and said "Hi dad, sorry we've not spent too much time together this week, but I've been very busy with work and school and other things . . . I'll see you later", I'd be understanding and tell him not to worry. Our relationship doesn't depend on us speaking to one another. The same is true with Anona, my best friend. There are intense times, times of discussion, social and sexual intercourse. And there are other times when we are just together – talking isn't necessary'.

Gerald Coates

To have such a God for a friend is something worth celebrating, and that, in a sentence, is what really strikes me about Gerald: he is a man who knows how to celebrate. Our interview was conducted during a busy leadership conference that he was addressing, and I asked him what his plans were when the conference was over.

'Well, I'll pick up a bottle of wine on the way home, and then I'll sit down with Anona, and we'll celebrate what we've been doing over the last forty-eight hours. I love to savour the good moments of life. So many people rush home after a great evening, when God was significantly working, only to punch the button on the television. We need to take time to enjoy the good moments, to be thankful, to gratefully bless God and one another.' Gerald is never happier than when celebrating. During a New Year's Eve meal with Cliff Richard, he stood in a restaurant and proclaimed a toast to 'the King and the Kingdom'. The entire restaurant raised their glasses – Gerald has wondered if they ever got round to wondering which king and which Kingdom they were honouring!

Perhaps this commitment to celebrate, this passion for thankfulness, is the reason for the remarkable mixture of the man that is Gerald Coates. He has been outspoken, probing and prophetic, and yet never cynical. He has been 'around the block' a few times and has seen his share of disappointments, but seems full of hope for the future. He is quick to smile, but will shed a tear easily when he talks about God or family or friends.

Our interview concluded and Gerald went off to raise another glass to life and love and the Lord of both. And I felt challenged to learn to drink a few toasts myself.

Sue Rinaldi

Finding God's heartbeat

Sue Rinaldi is a popular singer, songwriter, worship leader and communicator on contemporary issues.

It is Wednesday afternoon in the BBC's television studios in Wood Lane, Shepherd's Bush – time to record the following night's *Top of the Pops*.

In the dark, stuffy studio dozens of young revellers are all set to rave on cue when the 'On Air' sign lights up. Cameramen and sound technicians sit pensively by their equipment. Top disc jockeys Mike Smith and Janice Long check their scripts before introducing some of the country's leading bands.

In some cramped dressing-rooms nearby, artists are preparing to perform to millions of viewers on television's most popular music show. Some are smoking. Some are quiet. Some are having a drink.

Along the corridor, Christian band 'Heartbeat' are praying.

Among them is lead singer Sue Rinaldi, a spikey-haired girl and seemingly the sort you don't mess with.

'Lord, please help us,' she prays gently. 'We're really nervous. Help us to do well. And please, help people who watch us to see something of you in what we do'.

There is a knock on the door. It's Heartbeat's turn to perform. The song is 'Tears from Heaven', the single that had shot to number thirty-two in the charts. They leave their dressing room and walk onto the stage amid the smoke, noise and flashing coloured lights – taking the presence of the Living God with them.

For Sue, appearing on *Top of the Pops* was a dream come true. When she was eleven years old,

Friends of God

she picked up a guitar and decided she wanted to become a pop star, to get songs into the charts and appear on the smash-hit TV show. She wasn't a Christian then – and never dreamt that it would be God who made sure her dream was fulfilled. Now, more than twenty years later, she realizes that it was God who put those amibitions in her heart in the first place.

Six years after the *Top of the Pops* experience, she looks back on it wistfully and says: 'We had a real sense of God's presence with us as we sang our song. And I was personally very conscious of him – conscious that he was pleased that people were going to hear about him – conscious of his love for them – and conscious of his pleasure that I was fulfilling a deep ambition. It was very special.

'And it was brilliant being able to sing about God to millions of people who didn't know him, on *their* show. And what was really good was that after every TV show that Heartbeat did, the crew would come up to us and say what a pleasure it had been to work with us. Everyone was watching us carefully to see if we were "stereotype" Christians. I'm glad they found we weren't!'

Sue is a one-off. She is determined to avoid getting locked into the Christian music 'ghetto' and wants to break out of stereotyped Christian images and mix into the main music scene. She's never happier than when she's at the sharp end, confronting the way the church does things, asking the awkward questions, and striving to see 'relevant' Christianity being communicated. She loves being radical, being a non-conformer, breaking the rules.

When you look at her background, you can see why! She came from a non-Christian family and was tough. She walked the streets with the local

Sue Rinaldi

skinheads. She drank a lot. She went to all the wrong parties. She was a rebel.

Even after she became a Christian she carried on doing some of the wrong things – in fact she led the worship in her first church *before* she really gave her life to God! But gradually God got hold of her, changed her, even tamed her – but that rough-end, street-wise radical is still never far away!

Press the right buttons and she'll talk with grit, incisiveness and passion about the need for praise and worship songs to be musically, lyrically and culturally relevant, about the need for church meetings to genuinely relate to life and avoid the boredom factor, and about people who think that 'strong men' in churches are a blessing but who reject 'strong women' as manipulators.

But amid the brash radicalism there is a sensitive, caring woman who gets hurt easily . . . and who laughs her head off when describing how 'mega-rich' Heartbeat were so skint that all they had in the fridge the night before their *Top of the Pops* debut was two fish fingers!

Music is at the core of Sue's being. Music, music and more music. That's how she and God started out together. She began thinking about him when a visiting music team, including top Christian songwriter Graham Kendrick, visited her secondary school. Although she didn't become a Christian straight away, the team planted the seeds. And when she finally decided to throw her lot in with God, singing and music were right there from the outset.

She was already a good guitarist and had a powerful, penetrating voice, so she pointed her gifts God's way, leading worship, and touring coffee bars and youth groups – as ever, gravitating towards the rough, tough end of the human market. Although,

Friends of God

paradoxically, she was training to be an accountant, she started touring the country and working occasionally with leading Christian artists such as Ishmael and Dave Bilborough. And she formed her own band called 'Inside Out'.

In 1984, Sue's church in Southampton, then called Shirley Fellowship, and now known as City Gate, asked her to work for them full time, concentrating on music, schools work and evangelism. This gave her the chance to develop a national profile while keeping in touch with the local scene.

But God used this work to bring her to a musical crossroads. Her radical edge was on the line. It was decision time. She said: 'I couldn't understand why there was a Christian music scene on the one hand and then the rest of the music industry on the other. Why did we have to separate ourselves? What was the point? I wanted to get into the main stream of the music scene – to be a good singer who happened to be a Christian, like Cliff Richard and Amy Grant'.

Sue examined the options – and inevitably went the radical way. Her uncompromising nature gave her no choice! 'I was born that way,' she said. And that's where Heartbeat came in. Their hearts beat the way hers did. And when she signed for them in 1986 she soon found she shared their goals and dreams of musical excellence and their hunger for God. She took over as lead singer and worship leader, but she had to ask God to help her through a pain barrier. Sue, the solo artist, had to become Sue the team member.

Sue said: 'I was frightened because I thought I'd end up characterless! In fact, working with other people in Heartbeat didn't restrict me. It developed me'.

Sue Rinaldi

Sue also shared Heartbeat's dreams about getting out of the Christian music ghetto and into the mainstream musical market place. They realized that the charts were the only place to tap into the masses. So she helped write 'Tears from Heaven', the band found a producer and someone to promote the record. The single peaked at number 32 in the charts and opened the door to a flood of radio and TV interviews and articles in the national and musical press. Reports abounded of people who had heard about God's 'Tears From Heaven' . . . and been deeply moved.

Although the band were disappointed the song didn't make it into the top twenty, they followed 'Tears' with another chart single, 'The Winner', which Sue again co-wrote. It was an up-front praise number, and DJ Bruno Brooks loved it. It did well in the dance charts but sadly didn't rise above seventy in the main chart listings.

Sue quickly emerged as the group's spokeswoman and really made a name for herself on the BBC2 programme *Def II*. The programme was doing an A–Z of spiritual beliefs and asked representatives from different faiths to argue their case with a group of antagonistic, hostile youngsters. Sue, with her reputation of never being afraid of a scrap, was asked to represent Christianity and the new churches.

She said: 'I didn't know what I was letting myself in for! They gave me a "right grilling". I prepared myself as well as I could. I would never call myself a "theologian", but there I was in the role of an apologist for the Christian faith.

'But God turned up and helped me, and the programme went really well. The BBC received hundreds of letters from people who'd seen it – and nearly all of them were positive. I was amazed!

Friends of God

Since then the programme's been shown all over the world – even in the Australian outback! And it's led to me being asked to do similar kinds of events too. No-one's been more surprised than me!'

It's easy to simply label Sue as a take-'em-on zealot and look no further. To do so misses out the most important part of her radicalism. Her driving force is God. She wants to be as radical as he is. For the woman who appears on TV, sings in front of hundreds, gives press interviews, preaches and happily takes centre-stage only does so because she knows her God and really loves him. He's her father. As someone who never really felt fathered, she found this aspect of his nature quite hard to grasp. But once she experienced it, she came to treasure it – a parent figure who never fails.

God is also Sue's mate; she chats with him all the time and she doesn't mince her words with him when she's struggling.

When I met her in a plush hotel near Dorking, she was honest about the difficulties of leaving Heartbeat and re-adjusting to a new area, new friends and a new church. Change often brings insecurities and Sue felt that God had once again been challenging her in many areas of her life and thinking.

She said: 'When I was in Heartbeat, we really worked as a team, and obviously our life was pretty disciplined. We prayed, fasted, studied scripture and had input in a very organized way. But suddenly that disappeared. I was completely disorientated for a while. Once again I was a solo artist, needing personal motivation and an injection of direction. But my dreams have kept me going through crisis times'.

And has God been close during it all? As ever, Sue is very honest. 'I have never doubted that he's been

Sue Rinaldi

there, but it hasn't always been a bed of roses. He's been sorting me out on a lot of issues. It's been a time of reassessing. During 1992 my goals were to make friendships and settle into church life, to feel secure and to rediscover my own style in music again – one that would reflect my persona and influences and not the sound of Heartbeat.

'Another aspect is that I'm not married, so there's no constant factor in my life apart from God. Everything's changing all the time. I'm on a journey that never seems to end. I've also found it difficult to order my time without the discipline of team life to help me. I constantly need to re-address this in my daily life'.

Sue paused . . . reflected . . . and you wondered, momentarily, if that radical razor had gone blunt. Not for long. Her eyes blazed and she said: 'I'm still determined to fulfil the things that God has for me. My goal is still to achieve something artistically within the media . . . something that has a real touch of God about it.

'I want to write songs that are colourful, that make people think, that move people emotionally. I want to train the new generation of Christians to write songs that are current and relevant to society today, avoiding clichés and jargon. I want to see Christians leading the way in all kinds of areas in the arts and in life, with true integrity'.

Despite the struggles, Sue has worked out a system where she prays for a different subject each day. On Mondays she prays for the media, on Tuesdays for the Government, on Wednesdays, the Church, and so on. Most of her praying is done while she's out walking in the lush countryside which surrounds her home, or driving her car.

In terms of study, she's been attempting a Read

Friends of God

the Bible in a Year course during 1993 and she read plenty of books, mainly on topical issues. Her favourite? '*The Guinness Book of Poisonous Quotes!*' she laughs. 'Loads of tasty quotes about all aspects of life'.

Another item of essential reading for Sue is her Filofax. Not that she's a yuppie, it is just that she has got all the promises and prophecies that God has given her written down in it. And she reads them often, usually once a month . . . they've been one of the main ways she's been able to hold onto her dreams during a time of re-adjustment and change.

'I'm always motivated by my goals and by my dreams,' she says. 'One thing that has been said to me time and time again is that God's called me to be unique. I intend to stay that way. I can't be any other way! I want to get closer to God and go where he's leading me, although I haven't a clue where it'll be. On one hand I wanted to get married and have kids, and on the other, I love doing what I'm doing and would like to work much more within the media and make albums. Who knows?'

I asked Sue what she thought she'd be doing if she wasn't travelling as a singer/songwriter.

'Although I trained in accountancy, I think I'd give that a miss now! So I'd probably do something like work in a record shop, surrounded by music, or own a pub or a wine bar. But do you know, if I did, I'd be just as important to God. I'm not special to him because I've had profile. I'm important because I'm me.'

But she added: 'Whatever happens, I'm determined not to lose myself in mediocrity'.

Some chance! The future may be uncertain, but whatever it holds, this is one woman who can always be counted on to jump in with both feet!

Mike and Katey Morris

Two's company

Mike Morris is International Secretary of the Evangelical Alliance and a member of the Religious Liberty Commission of the World Evangelical Fellowship. Katey is a teacher and together the couple are on the leadership team of Revelation Church, Chichester, authors of a number of books and frequent speakers at Spring Harvest.

In the hustle and bustle of Heathrow airport's arrival lounge, a couple embrace one another . . . and pray together.

Globe-trotting freedom fighter Mike Morris has just returned from one of his frequent trips abroad, campaigning once again for religious liberty.

His devoted wife Katey is there to welcome him. And for the couple whose book *Praying Together* has helped so many people, a prayer at the airport is just as appropriate as a hug and a kiss when they meet up again.

Explains Mike: 'It might only be for thirty seconds or so, but to us it's an obvious thing to do. We're so pleased to see each other again that we stand and thank God'.

It is this kind of naturalness in prayer that has made Mike and Katey such a great help and example to thousands of married couples who have struggled to create any kind of spiritual life together.

And several years and 25,000 copies after the book first hit the shops, this homely couple are still practising what they preach – praying together and apparently enjoying it.

So what's the secret? Hasn't it become dull after all these years?

Said Mike, thirty-nine: 'Praying together has become more than a duty, and it's certainly never a chore. It's become part of every-day life, like eating together. We always approach prayer times with a sense of expectation. We enjoy them – they can be such exciting times!'

Mike and Katey Morris

One of the reasons Mike and Katey have achieved such naturalness in their prayer life is because they don't make a distinction between the secular and the spiritual.

They reckon that if they enjoy having dinner together and going shopping together – and they obviously do – then praying together is no different.

It wasn't always like this, though. Mike and Katey didn't hit on a prayer formula the day after they got married, write a book and then live happily ever after! They used to talk about anything and everything to avoid praying. They made the same mistake as many people and saw praying together as more important to God than the everyday things of life. This made it into a legalistic routine. And like all legalism it had no life in it and failed.

They didn't begin praying together until they'd been married for around two years. Katey was having a hard time in her job, and so they decided to pray about it. Then they started reading *Living Light* and their prayer times grew out of that. They have been going now for around twelve years – and they rarely miss a night. They reckon they pray together around 85 per cent of the times when they are at home together and Mike is not away.

So how does Mike and Katey's prayer life together actually work in practice? Well, it's all very ordinary! The walls of their three-bedroom home don't shake and God does not light up the sky over Chichester, where they live.

They simply pray together at around 10 p.m. to 10.30 p.m. – either just before they go to bed, or in bed – at the risk of going to sleep. And there have been plenty of times when the words have failed as sleep has engulfed them, and they have woken

Friends of God

up eight hours later to find the light still on and the Light of the world still waiting!

They normally read the Bible together and pray about things that are burdening them. Very often, their prayers will be of a global nature. One night they were deeply moved by pictures on *News at Ten* of a famine in Sudan. So they turned up Isaiah 53 and prayed about injustice and inequality in the world.

Said Katey: 'We also pray about issues in our own lives – things that have arisen during the day. I'm a teacher, and often have disruptive children to cope with. And we often find that after we pray for them, their behaviour changes. There was one particular boy who was about to join my class. He had a dreadful reputation and they'd had all kinds of trouble with him before. So we prayed together – and I can honestly say I've never had any trouble with him.

'We normally pray for ten or fifteen minutes. Sometimes we set an agenda, other times we just get straight into it. It varies. The day it becomes predictable is the day we'll struggle to keep going'.

But who takes the initiative? Katey grins broadly. 'Mike does, most of the time – not because he's The Man, but because he's that type of person, and that suits me fine. He's an initiator by nature. I'm not.

'He suggests that we pray and generally chooses the scripture that we read. We do anything to avoid being habitual. Once we prayed through the Anglican Prayer Book. Another times we used the *Imitation of Christ* by Thomas à Kempis. And during 1993 we're reading right through the Bible together. We're both really excited about that.'

But don't run away with the idea that everything is always sweetness and light in the Morris

Mike and Katey Morris

household! It's not. They don't glide through each day in a spiritual reverie before flating off on a prayer-cloud at bedtime.

Like any other couple, they're sometimes tetchy with each other. Sometimes they have rows. And the pressures on them, with Mike's travelling and their joint involvement in Revelation Church, are enormous. So on odd occasions the temptation is to ditch the prayer time. But they have an agreed commitment to reconciliation if they've had a row. And they challenge one another about the importance of their prayer time. 'We never let the sun go down on our anger,' said Katey.

Sometimes, Mike will want to pray and Katey won't – or the other way round. But they have worked hard to prevent such times creating a tense vacuum just before bedtime. If the person who doesn't want to pray is genuinely ill or tired or downcast, then the other person prays for them. But if they're 'swinging the lead' a bit, then the stronger partner at the time will challenge them. And if there's a mood or a bout of stroppiness causing problems, then they work together to resolve it before they start praying. They have successfully identified potential problem areas and devised strategies in advance on how to tackle them. It works.

Anyone who knows Mike and Katey will realize that they are very different from one another. Chalk and cheese would be an understatement! And these differences obviously show up in their prayer times together. Mike prefers to study scripture in a disciplined, systematic way, because he is that kind of person. But Katey enjoys meditating on a few verses and gaining inspiration from them.

Laughed Mike: 'At first we were very threatened

Friends of God

by each other's methods. I couldn't stand Kate's "butterfly approach". I didn't think it was sound! I used to give her long lectures about how she should change and do things my way. But now we both realize we can be enriched by one another's faith. I've learnt so much from Katey's approach, and she's benefited from the way I do things'.

Chipped in Katey: 'Over the years, we've become much more relaxed with each other. We've learned to appreciate each other's differences. Now, we can be having a conversation with each other in the car and suddenly get straight into prayer. Once we'd have been terribly embarrassed. I suppose you could say that your prayer life together is a very good reflection of your relationship as a whole. If you can pray naturally and honestly with one another, then there can't be too much wrong with your relationship'.

However, their prayer life has had to endure some very difficult problems over the years. Fairly early on in their marriage, they discovered that Katey could not have children. And more recently she was diagnosed as having multiple sclerosis. Both of these problems have tested their faith – and they are still waiting for God's healing, strong in the belief that it isn't far away now. But it hasn't been easy. Far from it.

Said Katey: 'I went through a time soon after I found I couldn't have children when I was so depressed that I didn't pray for three months. Prayer and bible study simply weren't on my agenda. I eventually came out of that, but it wasn't easy.

'The temptation is to ask God "Why?" But that's not helpful. You have to look at the benefits. Childlessness puts you in a crucible – it's given God the chance to speak into my life in a way that he

Mike and Katey Morris

wouldn't have been able to otherwise. And I'm so grateful for that'.

Mike is equally honest about the situation. Yes, there have been times when they've told God where to get off. Katey's problems caused pressure on the marriage and he recalls the dark times when she felt a failure both as a wife and in terms of her femininity. But they both discovered facets to God's personality in all the hardship.

Mike explained: 'We discovered that God is happy to be confronted. We have learnt to be very honest with him and with each other. Yes, we have both been broken over the childlessness issue at times. Once I collapsed in my friend Clive Calver's arms and cried for several hours. But in all that, God was there, bringing healing and releasing hope.'

Mike has found that one of the hardest things to bear, with both the childlessness issue and now Katey's health, has been that it is her, and not him, on the receiving end of the problems. He is a problem solver by nature. He has generally succeeded in most of the challenges that life's thrown at him – but in both these situations, he was completely powerless to do anything at all.

So what did they do – and what are they still doing in the situation? Like most people in one sphere or another, they are hanging on to God's promises with as much faith as they can muster.

Soon after Katey's multiple sclerosis was diagnosed, they went to see John Barr, an Elim minister with a recognized healing and deliverance ministry. He told them that they had to treat the illness as an enemy, and fight it out. If they didn't, it could be something that could destroy their ministry and their lives together.

Friends of God

So that's what they did – and are still doing today. They pray for healing and for children most nights. They meet with friends regularly to call out on God for a breakthrough. A group of close friends recently got together and prayed and fasted for Katey for three days. People from all over the country regularly intercede for her. And they keep on believing. And not without good reason.

They feel that God has been good to them right through the childlessness problem by constantly giving them promises about a future – with a family.

Faith Forster prophesied they would have children. And Ian Andrews, who did not know anything about Katey's condition, prophesied that she would have twins – a word they say that has been confirmed several times since. And the American prophet Dale Gentry prophesied to Mike and Katey that they would have a house that would be filled with children. Other people regularly write to them, giving words of hope and encouragement. Many people have had dreams about Katey – and twins seem to be a recurring theme. Her sister has them – so why should she miss out?

It is these words, and God's proven love to them, that have given them the courage and the determination to keep going, even when there is no sign of answered prayer.

Mike explained: 'We would rather go to the grave believing for children than attempt to rationalize the situation or accept it. We will always believe God in it all. His word gives us no choice!

'And the irony of it all is that we have often prayed for other couples who are childless – and God has healed them. They have ended up having children and we still can't have any! We have to laugh! We think it must be God's way of encouraging us to keep

Mike and Katey Morris

going. We just keep on hoping and praying that he'll do the same for us soon'.

Adds Katey with a laugh: 'And the emphasis is on the word *soon*! After all, I am thirty-eight now! I'm going to be old enough to be a granny before long! What will the other mothers at the school think!'

Whatever the future holds, one thing is for certain. Mike and Katey will keep holding onto God and his promises with that rare blend of reality and humour. And without sounding syrupy or sentimental, they'll keep doing what they've done for so many years now – praying together.

Fran Beckett

A father found

Fran Beckett is head of the Shaftesbury Society's Urban Action division and manager of fifty-two church-based community action projects in Greater London.

Fran Beckett never knew her real father and was raised by her mum and grandmother.

As a child she dreamed of having an ideal father: someone who had plenty of time for her, someone who was always there when she needed him, someone who loved her and believed in her.

In a way, the dream came true. During her late teens Fran became a Christian and discovered God, the father figure she had always pictured – only better.

Now forty-one, Fran said: 'Up until then, a father was someone who didn't want me, someone who went away and left me. But God turned that right round. The first thing I learnt about God when I became a Christian was his father heart.

'I think that's quite unusual. Most people tend to get to know Jesus first, but I was different. And the most wonderful thing was that I discovered that God fulfilled that childhood dream of a model father. Maybe that dream was put in my heart by God himself. Who knows? But it never left me'.

Ever since she became a Christian, Fran's been trying to express his love to the needy – to life's victims – people who have suffered hurts.

She is currently head of Urban Action with the Shaftesbury Society. That means she oversees fifty-two church-based social action projects in London, ranging from senior citizens' lunch clubs to a homeless initiative for young people.

Before she went into full-time Christian work, Fran worked as a social worker, helping the mentally

Friends of God

ill, people with learning disabilities and others in crisis situations.

So caring for others has always been a priority. Why? Simply because other people cared for her before she was a Christian. A Christian family took her under their wing during her teens and literally 'loved her into God's kingdom'. They didn't preach good news to her. They didn't have to. They *were* good news. In the end she genuinely wanted to become a Christian – she had seen the reality of it in action. It was their practical caring that attracted her to Christ's message, not their words.

Said Fran: 'Since then I've done my best to care for people. My vision is to see the church *be* good news like this family was to me. Unless we are, people will never take us seriously'.

Fran's encounter with God was not an isolated event in her teens and she's hungry to know him even better – to the extent that she recently spent several weeks studying Psalm 142, where the writer describes how 'his soul was panting after God's presence.' She feels a similar urgency and desire to know God.

She explained: 'There is tremendous pressure these days to substitute relationship with God with activity. It's a twentieth-century problem and I am just as susceptible to it as anybody. Everyone's more occupied with doing than with being.

'A relationship with God is something that has to develop naturally. But there are still active steps you can take to check the imbalances. So I am trying to be more disciplined in my bible reading and in the time I spend with God. I am trying to spend time with him every day, even if it's a brief time'.

Spending time with God means a two-way conversation and Fran is always conscious of the

Fran Beckett

need to hear from God as well as to speak to him. But how does that work out in practice? How does she hear God?

She said: 'God has spoken to me in many different ways. I have never seen angels or heard him speak audibly or anything like that. When you read in scripture about people hearing directly from God like that or even seeing him, it's awe-inspiring. I don't think I could cope with an experience like that. Even Moses had to hide behind a rock as God walked by, so what chance would I stand?

'But when I pray I often feel a strong sense of the warmth of his love and he speaks to me through scripture – words leap out of the Bible at me and have a profound effect on me'.

Fran is aware of God's presence with her at work – and when she's out walking on the beach or through the woods. It is at times like these that he sometimes reveals things to her.

And she feels she can relate to God in two different ways. There are prayers which she sends up in the daily rush of life. Then there are the 'QTs' . . . but she doesn't call them Quiet Times. Fran prefers 'Quality Times' – times which she sets aside to be alone with God. These are disciplined, rather like her upbringing. For over the years Fran has discovered that you can't develop a relationship with anybody – human or God – without devoting quality time to it. So she spends an hour in prayer and reflection two or three times a week. These slots can be at any time of the day – but rarely in the mornings!

She said: 'I struggle in the early mornings. A lot of people say it is spiritual to get up and pray early. They tell you that they feel marvellous for the rest of the day. I don't. I feel dreadful'.

Friends of God

Finding opportunities to pray at work is not always easy when you go from one meeting to another and deal with a host of secular groups and agencies.

Fran admits: 'Shaftesbury is a link between the church and the world, and when you are dealing with local councils and secular groups there is always a pressure to compromise. But when I'm having meetings with my staff or with people who are involved in our churches and projects, I insist on praying with them every time – not to rubber-stamp decisions, but to allow God the space and the opportunity to speak and to guide us where necessary. My aim is to keep God central in all that I do.

'I'm currently devising a financial strategy for my work – we have had some very real financial problems. But it will be a prayerful strategy.

'I've seen some wonderful answers to prayers at work. There have occasionally been difficult situations, where there's hostility and confusion. But after praying I've seen God change the whole situation around with no human intervention. You can't explain things like that, but it's so exciting seeing God care about everyday problems'.

Fran writes a lot of her prayers rather than saying them. For her, writing them out works just as well.

She explained: 'I've got books at home containing prayers that I've written to God. I'm a words on paper person, and I find it easy to communicate with him that way. Why not? After all, we write letters to other people we love. Why should we treat God any differently?'

Fran is blunt and honest with God, both when she writes to him and when she speaks to him. She loves the Psalms, where the writers are frank about their

Fran Beckett

fears, their anger, their uncertainties and their joys.

'There's no point in pretending,' she says. 'But most of us aren't honest all the time. We easily kid ourselves. But God likes to hear it like it is. I always encourage others to be as honest as possible with God. That doesn't mean you'll always get answers, but hurts and frustrations and anger are always better expressed than not'.

Bible reading also plays a significant part in Fran's quality times. She tends to be quite methodical in the way she studies scripture, and isn't a 'dot-around' reader.

But having said that, she likes variety and tends to change her method of study every few months. She's used Scripture Union notes, the Crusade for World Revival 'Read the Bible in a Year' course. At other times she has done a bible study on a particular word, and used a concordance to find that word right through from Genesis to Revelation. Once she did a study on the word 'Joy' – and ended up not just knowing what it meant, but being a lot more joyful too!

She also has whole days when she goes away and spends time praying, studying, worshipping, meditating, singing to God and speaking in tongues.

The fact that she prays in tongues might surprise people who feel that the charismatic gifts and social action don't go together. Well, sometimes they don't – but with Fran, they do. And she sometimes sees a picture in her mind and is aware that God is saying something through it.

Fran is not a lady who can be easily pigeon-holed. She breaks all the rules and preconceptions. She is a Spirit-filled, evangelical – and yet is firmly committed to social action.

And then she's a woman, and not only that, but

Friends of God

a woman who's a leader. And a woman who is the 'boss' to a number of men. And on top of that, she's single!

Her eyes twinkled as she said: 'I'm a bit of a one-off! Because I go to Ichthus, a house church in London, I embrace the charismatic wing of the church. But I also work with people from all types of backgrounds, some of whom are definitely not charismatic. Happily, though, being in Ichthus is a distinct advantage, because they are probably as heavily involved in social action as many 'liberal' churches.

'Then on top of being a woman leader, I must be one of the few single women who is nationally known! Others, such as Faith Forster, are married. It's an enormous privilege, having God use me to break some of the rules. But it's an enormous burden at times. I wouldn't say that I've been personally criticized for doing what I do, but I am sometimes aware that it's there in the background'.

Despite the criticisms and the hurts that Fran's been through in her ministry, a sense of humour is never far from her. She has a warm face that smiles easily and is ready to dissolve into laughter at the least opportunity. It's probably her ability to laugh at life's problems and see the funny side of difficult issues that has helped her to handle such a big workload.

She enjoys life and she speculates excitedly about whether there will be Indian food, red wine, decent coffee and endless supplies of chocolate in heaven. And she laughs again as she describes her encounters – with a God who laughs too.

She said: 'There are many times where God reminds me of how *he* sees a situation. It might be something that I'm really up-tight about, but then

Fran Beckett

I become aware of how he sees it – and I just can't help laughing. It's very therapeutic!

'Other people experience the Holy Spirit through visions or words of knowledge, but just occasionally I experience a great release of joy and laughter. It's never when I expect it, but it does remind me that God has a sense of humour and that he can bring great relief from pressure by laughing with us'.

As Fran chats away in her modern office in a busy south London street, you start to realize that her relationship with God is a very rich tapestry. It's not one you can pigeon-hole. It is deep and varied.

But one thing is for certain – she knows the God who revealed himself to her all those years ago extremely well. And those who meet her are all the richer for it.

Steve Chalke

Beating the clock

The Baptist Evangelist Steve Chalke has spearheaded numerous initiatives including Oasis Trust, Christmas Cracker and Radio Cracker. He also appears on the ITV programme Sunday Morning.

It is 5.44 in the morning, and all is quiet in Steve Chalke's darkened home. Emily, Daniel, Abigail and Joshua are tucked up in bed, blissfully unaware of the rude awakening that is about to happen down the hall in mum and dad's bedroom . . . and then at 5.45 a.m. precisely, the sleepy silence is shattered by what Steve describes with feeling as an 'evil sounding' alarm clock, a shrill ring that demands a response. Quickly, lest the whole family be disturbed, Steve slaps the clock – and another day begins.

And it's likely to be a busy day too. Just reading through the list of Steve Chalke's responsibilities wore me out. Director of the fast growing Oasis Trust. Lead person in the successful Christmas Cracker campaign, which has raised millions for the poor and hungry. Member of the Baptist Union Council. Member of the Evangelical Alliance Executive. One of the directors and an executive member of Spring Harvest. Itinerant evangelist, easily the best-known youth speaker in Britain. Author of a number of books and a monthly magazine feature. Oh, and I almost forgot – in his spare time he oversees two Baptist Churches; all this as well as being husband to Cornelia (who is hopefully able to sleep through loud alarm-clock-type noises at 5.46 a.m.!) and father of four. In fact Steve is so busy and in demand that he has a diary committee that helps him sift through the many invitations that pour in. And so much does he love his work, that he admits that he finds it difficult to

Friends of God

switch off – even when on holiday. 'I'm always reading, always thinking, dreaming up new ideas . . .'

So what's busy Steve doing getting up at 5.45 a.m. in the morning? He is eager to dismiss any idea of 'super sainthood' which I am immediately tempted to tag him with. 'Of course I don't do it every morning – there are times when I don't get home until 1 or 2 a.m. from preaching somewhere, and then it would be ridiculous to try to maintain that schedule. And then there are times like Spring Harvest which completely upset my schedule and tend to wipe my spiritual disciplines out'. (I sigh a deep sigh of relief: we are chatting together at Spring Harvest, and early morning prayer is the last thing on my personal agenda while there!)

'It's just that this is the pattern which I try to follow – most mornings'.

Despite his obvious humility, I'm still impressed, and eager to know just exactly how he got into this early waking habit.

He laughed, and followed through quickly with that broad smile that seems to occupy every square inch of his face: 'Well, I went to a meeting where a fairly well-known Baptist minister was sharing how he got up early every morning to pray, and I really felt challenged by his discipline, so I decided to adopt the pattern myself. The ironic thing is that, a year later, I went for a meal in the home of that same inspiring minister, and I told him how much he had encouraged me. His wife laughed out loud, turned to her husband and said "Oh yes dear, that was the week that you got up early to pray for a few days and then went off to that leaders' gathering and told them it was now your habit – it only lasted the week, didn't it?".'

Steve Chalke

Yet still Steve keeps the practice going, when he knows that his inspiring friend probably sleeps as he rises. Is he bound up in chains of legalism, desperately trying to please God by getting up while it's dark?

Another smile, wry this time.

'No, although I have to say that I went through a very legalistic phase in my Christian life in the early years – it was just awful. I was committed to the "Daily Quiet Time" as an act of slavery. I'd read through the Bible once a year because I just *had to*; I was wading through guilt as well as scripture. Now I've come to realize that God isn't into that: I can pray at all times, and prayer is an attitude as well as an action. I used to believe that God couldn't use anyone unless they were totally disciplined – and that's just not true, because he's chosen to use me. In fact if he only used the perfectly disciplined, not too many people would be used by God!'

This early legalism also reared its ugly head when Steve was considering what God wanted him to do. 'I'd been raised on the idea that God's will for your life is probably what you don't want to do – so if you hate the idea of going to the mission field, that's obviously what God has got up his sleeve, as it were, for you. I also believed that *everybody* had to have some major call from God, some blinding revelation. I just made up my mind one day, while at Spurgeon's College, that I really wanted to be an evangelist. I felt excited by the idea, it seemed to be in line – but there was only one trouble – I didn't "have a verse", a scripture had not "jumped out at me", and moreover, I actually *wanted* to be an evangelist – which meant that it had to be wrong!

'I was terrified – and massively depressed. It was only when I became convinced that God was

Friends of God

speaking to me through my own desires that I felt released to move forward into what I'm doing now'.

Okay, okay, so Mr. Chalke isn't given to 40,000 revelations a day, and isn't bound up by legalism, so why not consign the evil alarm clock to the bin?

'Basically, I want to say and do what God wants me to say and do – and with my busy lifestyle, I need to set aside some time to get alone with him – plus the way that I pray prevents me from getting locked up in what I'm doing, helps me keep things in focus'.

Not that the daily routine means that praying has become easy. Steve still finds concentrating on prayer difficult. 'My mind wanders a lot, and I'm easily distracted, so I walk round our lounge, make myself a cup of tea, make a fuss of the cat, and in the midst of all of that, try to keep my prayer conversational – a chat with God. Sometimes the distinction between my own thoughts and what I want to say in prayer becomes a bit blurred'.

To help focus his concentration, Steve lines the walls of his study with pictures of friends who are serving God in different parts of the world. 'I don't use prayer lists simply because I tend to lose them, which isn't very helpful! I do find that my photographs help me, otherwise my prayers could get too parochial and "me orientated", and they give me a handle on praying for "the whole world". It's difficult to meaningfully pray for the entire planet, but my pictures help me focus onto specific people and projects that are important. I also find that praying for people helps me in my relationships with them – it's difficult to gossip about someone that you pray for every day'.

As someone who has found concentrating on reading scripture quite a challenge early in the morning (and some parts of it have been an uphill climb at any time of the day!) I was intrigued to know the Steve Chalke approach to the Bible, and hearing the voice of God generally.

It turns out that he is addicted to commentaries! 'I find *The Bible Speaks Today* series really helpful, and I love anything that John Stott turns out. I've just finished a whole year of studying 2 Timothy with Mr. Stott, via his excellent commentary book.

'As far as hearing God speaking to me is concerned, I've never heard an audible voice or anything like that. Most of the time God seems to speak to me through repetition – everywhere I look, the same idea or concept seems to appear and reappear – whether it's through reading Scripture, or as happened one time, through reading *Woman's Own* in the doctor's waiting room!' (I sighed with relief at this point, grateful that I'm not the only Christian male who reads ladies' periodicals in waiting rooms!)

'I try to listen to others whom I know are sensitive to God as well – my wife, Corny, for example. Often she'll say "I think that you should be doing this . . ." and I'd be a fool not to listen to her, she has lots of wisdom.

'And I do try to make sure that I take note of what God says to me. Section nine in my Filofax is my "What has God said?" section, and I write things down and often refer back to them. After all, if God has taken the trouble to say something, it's important to take notice, isn't it?'

So with all this talk of godly spouses filled with wisdom, one might think that the Chalke household is a Baptist version of *The Waltons*, with everyone gathering around as daddy opens the giant leather family Bible (brass hinges standard equipment) and

Friends of God

chorusing their prayers last thing at night . . . 'Goodnight John boy, Goodnight Corny, Goodnight Jesus!'

Again Steve rushes to puncture the potential myth. 'Sounds nice, but it just isn't that way. Our lifestyle doesn't allow us to pray together and read scripture as much as I'd like to. We talk about the Lord together very naturally, and more often than not end up discussing and praying about the issues that concern us, but it's not anything like every day – though Emily and Daniel really enjoy the young people's version of *Every Day with Jesus*, which is great. We want them to develop their faith without us pushing anything down their throats. Surveys taken among Christian families have shown quite clearly that teenagers do a lot better when they haven't had Jesus forced on them – we try to remember that'.

Our interview had lasted quite a while by now, and Steve had been kind enough to let me in on some of his own personal habit patterns. But I wanted to go deeper, to try to find out, not just what he did, but who he is. Does super efficient, smooth-talking Chalke have his low spots – is he vulnerable?

I was surprised, and grateful for his honesty. He told me about some of the loneliness of his work – how he needs liberal doses of encouragement. 'It's ironic really. People know that I have something of a reputation as a communicator, so they don't think that I need to hear any feedback or affirmation if I did a reasonable job when I preach! It's as if they think that I have reached a point where I don't need to hear any positive words any more'.

Of course the real truth is, that just like the rest of us, Steve has his fair share of struggles and insecurities. Which of us has never felt dwarfed by

Steve Chalke

someone else's abilities and gifting? Perhaps remarkably for one so obviously gifted, Steve still occasionally struggles with comparing himself negatively with others. And he has his low times emotionally. 'I suppose that about 25 per cent of my life I feel really close to God, 50 per cent of the time I feel just OK, and about 25 per cent of the time I find myself feeling a bit stale and fed up'. He is encouraged by the fact that even the great C. H. Spurgeon battled with roller-coaster emotions, occasionally turning to a nip of gin before preaching in order to lift his flagging spirits!

So what keeps Steve going?

'The fact that the gospel is true is what keeps me going – I refuse to be driven by the fickleness of my own feelings. You see, I've thought this whole thing through very carefully. I'm a very logical person. The fact is that Jesus really is who he claimed to be – and that fact can't be changed by my having an occasional emotionally rainy day. What's true is true, and I've committed my life to serve that truth – and that's that!'

That simple logic has motivated Steve to embrace the manic schedule of activity that he lives with today – and his heroes are all men and women of action and passion. 'I admire people like Mother Teresa, and Martin Luther King, because they have lived their beliefs. It was King who said, "You're never truly alive until you know what you'd die for" '.

He is also grateful to others who have exercised a great influence on his life, for example, Steve Flashman. 'Steve actually gave me the opportunity in the early days to get out of the pew and *do* something. It had a powerful effect on my life. That's why I love to develop projects that will enable

Friends of God

young people to actually roll up their sleeves and get involved with affecting the world, rather than just talking about change!'

Writers like C. S. Lewis, and A. W. Tozer, and firebrands like C. T. Studd and Leonard Ravenhill, (*Why revival tarries*) also figure as major influences.

I came away from my interview with Steve Chalke with a fresh understanding of why it is that God is using him so powerfully. It is because he is just Steve Chalke – no pretences, no pseudo-spirituality, no haloes; with his big smile and matching heart, a thoroughly good bloke! He knows his own weaknesses: 'I don't suppose I've ever done anything because of 100 per cent pure motives', and he knows the heart of God: 'God has often reminded me that he wants me to have my priorities right – if I develop a craving for fame, then he will withhold it from me, for my own good!'

An ordinary guy, and an instrument of God.

But then, God only uses ordinary people as his instruments.

A last word

Fourteen leading Christians, all apparently enjoying the smile and blessing of God upon their lives – and all working out their friendship with him differently. If we were looking for a foolproof formula, a definitive method to help us to walk with God, we'd be disappointed. But we shouldn't be surprised.

After all, true Christianity isn't a mere religion, it's a friendship, and variety and creativity are essential elements to any friendship. Pick half a dozen people and ask them to tell you how they approach their human relationships and you'll probably get half a dozen different answers. I would have been worried if the friends of God that I met had all been robotically similar. Their lifestyles differ, as does their churchmanship. There are Anglicans, Baptists, Methodists, Charismatics – what they do on Sunday differs widely!

What is consistently true of all fourteen is that they all love God supremely – Jesus is number one in their lives, and that issue has been settled long ago. They have all paid a price for the faith. They have all been unashamed to declare that Jesus is their Lord. Not all of them start their day with a quiet time – but every one of them has decided that each and every moment of every day should be spent glorifying God. All are agreed that walking with God – however you do that – is the key to a successful life. Be encouraged by their honesty. Be inspired by their tenacity. If you think that one of their ideas might work for you, steal it, and give it a try!

Friends of God

But most of all, realize your uniqueness, and don't get locked into other people's methods. One thing, and one thing only is important – that you and I walk with the God who calls us to be faithful. The outworking of that faithfulness on a daily basis will be a unique adventure!

There will come a day when all the friends of God will be gathered together around the Friend himself. People of every tribe and tongue, of every era and cultural background . . . celebrating the best friend that they ever met, the One who sticks closer than a brother: Jesus. Prayer will be obsolete, for we'll see him face to face. No longer will we peer through the gloom with the eyes of faith, all will be revealed.

Until that day – be a faithful friend of God. And if you haven't met Jesus yet, if you haven't become a Christian, why not get introduced? He'd love to be your friend . . . and to have you as one of his.